Friend,
Books feed
body and spirit...
Thank you for your supp'r.
[signature]
5/7/2023

Brentwood Literary Stroll

Look! I Can Fly

Perseverance Is My Superpower
PART I

••••••••••• An Autobiography •••••••••••

D. J. Wilson

iUniverse

LOOK! I CAN FLY
AN AUTOBIOGRAPHY

Copyright © 2022 D. J. Wilson.

All rights reserved. No part of this book may be used or reproduced by any means, graphic, electronic, or mechanical, including photocopying, recording, taping or by any information storage retrieval system without the written permission of the author except in the case of brief quotations embodied in critical articles and reviews.

The views expressed in this work are solely those of the author and do not necessarily reflect the views of the publisher, and the publisher hereby disclaims any responsibility for them.

iUniverse books may be ordered through booksellers or by contacting:

iUniverse
1663 Liberty Drive
Bloomington, IN 47403
www.iuniverse.com
844-349-9409

Because of the dynamic nature of the Internet, any web addresses or links contained in this book may have changed since publication and may no longer be valid. The views expressed in this work are solely those of the author and do not necessarily reflect the views of the publisher, and the publisher hereby disclaims any responsibility for them.

Any people depicted in stock imagery provided by Getty Images are models, and such images are being used for illustrative purposes only. Certain stock imagery © Getty Images.

Look! I Can Fly depicts true actual events that occurred throughout the author's early life. The book is written from her point of view, and it is based on the author's personal experiences, knowledge, observation, and memories of said events. The characters within do represent actual individuals, but the names, including her own, places, physical properties, businesses, and places of residences have been changed or omitted, in an effort, to protect privacy.

Holy Bible, New Living Translation, copyright © 1996, 2004, 2015 by Tyndale House Foundation. Used by permission of Tyndale House Publishers, Inc., Carol Stream, Illinois 60188. All rights reserved.

ISBN: 978-1-6632-4415-4 (sc)
ISBN: 978-1-6632-4414-7 (e)

Library of Congress Control Number: 2022916784

Print information available on the last page.

iUniverse rev. date: 10/14/2022

To my parents – whose sacrifices paved the way for me to achieve the earthly things that they only dream about.

And

Chloe – a special daughter, any parent would be proud to call a progeny.

Don't judge by his appearance or his height, for I have rejected him. The Lord doesn't see things the way you see them. People judge outward appearance, but the Lord looks at the heart.

—1 Samuel 16:7 NLT

Preface

Look! I Can Fly depicts true actual events that occurred throughout my early life. The book is written from my point of view, and it is based on my personal experiences, knowledge, observation, and memories of said events. The characters within do represent actual individuals, but the names, including my own, places, physical properties, businesses, and places of residences have been changed or omitted, in an effort, to protect privacy.

• •

The first eighteen years of my life read like a best-selling novel. It included dark family secrets, controversy, extreme situations, action, and consequences. The problem was that my heart lacked the courage and desire to tell my story. The tools needed to deal with this sad, and painful truth were hidden deep in my mind, waiting to be discovered. It was the stuff that the blues singers of my childhood sang about. The blues, a genre of music that used poverty, hard work, heartache, hardship, oppression, depression, and loss to shed light on the conditions of the poor, mostly people of color living in the southeastern part of the United States.

The Mississippi Delta gave birth to a long list of notable blues musicians and singers, including the man called the King of the Blues, B. B. King. Through this music, they introduced generations of people around the world to the plight of poor Black people in the Jim Crow South. My parents, and my maternal ancestors were born into poverty in the State of Mississippi. They worked as farm laborers in the cotton industry, and earned pennies compared to the true value of their work. A life of drudgery and servitude was destined to be their fate, and that of their descendants.

My mother and others of her age group loved the blues. When she heard a song she liked, she grabbed a broom, or an imaginary prop to slow danced around the room. She was a good singer, so she sang along with the record, as her facial expressions changed with the emotions of the lyrics. She connected with every word of a song, and the lyrics went somewhere deep in her soul. At that time, I didn't understand the music, or why anyone else liked it. I thought it was for people like my parents. To me, the music was scary, loud, too sad, and depressing.

I once asked Mom, "What's so special about the blues?"

"Just keep on living," she said.

By the time I turned fifteen, most of the traumatic, life-altering events described in this book had occurred. And by the age of eighteen, my appreciation for the music that I disliked so much in my youth, had changed. Because by then, I had done a lot of living. And all of the ingredients that makes up the blues, were now part of my life experiences.

My first experience with heartache occurred when I was sixteen. While hospitalize for an illness with an uncertain prognosis, my best girlfriend and my boyfriend began an intimate relationship. The treachery was revealed by another girlfriend. Their disloyalty, and unfaithfulness, stung deep. When I allowed myself to trust again, my next high school boyfriend, openly cheated, and was verbally and physically abusive. He was crazy jealous and possessive, and reminded me of my father in a bad way. Not only did I watch my mother's domestic violence abuse, I have my own story to tell.

Living below the federal poverty level sealed my fate. Poverty was the hallmark for a life filled with hardship, oppression, depression, and hard work. Both of my parents worked as farm laborers, but didn't earn a living wage. I watched them struggle and worry about our future needs. To help them, while still in high school, I worked part-time as a maid and babysitter, earning less than $15 a week. That work was dehumanizing, demeaning, degrading, and I was treated with disrespect. It was a traumatic experience, and it caused me to have phobias as it related to germs and cleanliness to present day. To avoid working as a domestic, I chopped cotton. What I learned from this experience as a domestic worker - don't ask others to do for you, that you wouldn't do for yourself; be kind and respectful in all situations; and know your worth.

During the summer, I chopped cotton. This was hard work, even for a young person like me. Blisters and corns formed on the inside of my hands from gripping the hoe - the tool used to remove weeds from around the cotton. The work was exhausting, because one had to walked all day, and it caused my feet to hurt. My work shoes were not sufficient for the amount of walking the work required. The awkward motion used to remove the weeds, caused backaches. Exposure to the hot sun, with only a straw hat and a long sleeve shirt for protection, caused awful sunburns and skin rashes. Some of the field workers covered up so well, they resemble a mummy.

At mid-day, we were allowed a lunch break. I found the closest tree or shrub and collapsed under it. The older workers continued to stand using their hoe for support, as one older gentleman put it, "If I get down there, it's gon' take all y'all to get me up." Needless to say, the pay was awful, and provided no benefits.

The work was intense, but boring. Conversations between the workers were discouraged, because the landowner or the straw boss wanted us to focus on weed removal. Talking was a cause to get fired. To break the tedious repetitions, and the awful silence, someone would sing, or maybe someone would have a transistor radio. In the field, the radio only picked up one station - country music. If a chopper complained about the selection, someone would say, "It's the same as the blues, just sung by White folks." Chopping cotton required both hands on the hoe. The person with the transistor radio tapped it around the neck, or to the top of the straw hat, otherwise, we wouldn't be able to hear it.

The difficult times opened my eyes to life, and helped me

understand the blues genre of music, and its importance to the African-American culture.

As a child growing up in the rural Mississippi Delta, I wished for indoor plumbing, and a quiet and safe place to sleep. Indoor plumbing would have alleviated the need to carry water from an outdoor pump to the house. We used the water for everything—drinking, bathing, cooking, washing clothes, washing dishes, and cleaning the floors. Not an easy task, but we did it. Dad kept the outhouse looking good on the outside, but it was an awful experience to use it, because the smell couldn't be avoid. It was dehumanizing and degrading, but a common structure in the backyards of poor people, living on farms in rural communities in the South. Worst of all, we had to be on guard for snakes, because they sometimes took refuge in that place too.

Instead of achieving the desires of a little girl's heart, I had to face the reality of life. There would be no rest at night because of the frequency of domestic violence. Discrimination, bullying, and domestic terrorism contributed to my constant state of fear and worry. Violent crime, a common occurrence during the Civil Rights Movement of the 1950s and 1960s. It claimed the lives of private citizens, political and civil rights leaders. I was always afraid, and feared for the safety of my family. The fear of the bad men coming in the night caused me stress and worry. It was a difficult time to be born, and a turbulent time to live.

The Vietnam War had a negative impact on me also. The war claimed the lives of thousands of young men, including some from my small community. The war stole the hearts and souls of our families. The government used the draft, the mandatory enrollment of individuals into the armed forces, to fight a war that most US citizens didn't understand or support. The war took young Black men from the cotton fields to the battlefield. Several of my cousins were drafted. Some survived the madness of war, but others made the ultimate sacrifice—death. The ones that made it home, brought the madness with them, as they suffered physical and mental health issues. But some of them chose drugs and alcohol to cope with the trauma of war. Seeing how much the war took from them, made me sad.

The incidences of domestic violence were the most difficult for me to come to grips with. It was a very dark family secret that haunted me for as long as I can remember. It was a horrible experience to witness as a child, and to personally experience as a teenager. It negatively impacted my self-worth, confidence, and identity as a person. My hope was to suppress these memories forever. Domestic violence stopped me from moving forward with this project, as I couldn't figure out how to tell my story, exclude the domestic violence, and still be true to myself.

Bullying was another tough subject that I had to reconcile with before deciding to write this book. But with time, I made peace with this past injustice. Sadly, the problem of bullying didn't end with me, five decades ago. Society ignored this problem, and now this bad behavior, occurs openly in entertainment, politics, sports, on the job, at home, in school, and in our everyday lives. Fifty years ago, fear and low self-esteem caused me to suffer in silence, but I have found my voice, and decided to use it to say, "Stop it! It's wrong, it's mean, it hurts, and it's a crime." Hurt people hurt other people.

Moreover, depression, sadness, and the shame that I harbored in my spirit, about the life that I was born into, and the traumatic events that I endured, further hindered me from telling my story. However, the excuses that I used to not put pen to paper are no more. Fate intervened, when the world was forced to shut down and shelter in place as COVID-19 took hold. Alone, lonely, no place to go, and nothing to do at this late hour of the night. Twiddling my thumbs, scrolling through the menu on the television for what seemed like an hour, but nothing of interest caught my eye. I settled on the Weather Channel for entertainment.

To my surprise, the Holy Spirit whispered, "This is your time to write." The words filled my brain like a computer downloading information. My brain pushed back, the old excuses and fears about writing returned. It was all happening so fast—the words, phrases, and sentences all screaming to get out. With all that going on in my head, my hand grabbed a pen and paper and started writing. My hand could barely keep up with the increased traffic in my head. That first night turned into a marathon that continued until dawn. After that, I wrote every waking moment. The first draft of this manuscript was completed in about a week. God took the reins, and used me as His instrument to tell this story, which had been shelved for many years.

My spirit felt at peace, after introducing domestic violence and bullying in the book. I had to come to terms with my own demons, before, I could understand the problems and decisions of others. This journey taught me that birth doesn't guarantee you a certain standard of living, a cohesive and loving family, an inheritance, or the freedom to become successful. In the real world, birth doesn't guarantee you anything. You have to fight every day for your right to exist. Life is not like in the movies, where you can write a Hollywood ending. For most people, life is like a thicket filled with thorns. You can accept the situation and stay stuck, or wake up each day determined to plow your way through it, one inch at a time.

Look! I Can Fly is part I of my autobiography. It's my story of a life wrought with disappointment, uncertainty, hardship, violence, and fear. This book, the first in a series, tells how those experiences helped shape my life; and how hope and perseverance led me through the tough times. In subsequent books, the path used to escape a troubled past, and how a tiny speck of courage changed my life will be shared. I hope you find this book interesting, informative, entertaining, and thought provoking.

Contents

Preface ix
Introduction xix

Chapter 1   In the Beginning 1
Chapter 2   The Perils of Living on a Farm 7
Chapter 3   Saved by Grace 12
Chapter 4   Unaccompanied Minors...................................23
Chapter 5   When Weather Becomes a Foe 28
Chapter 6   Turbulent Social and Economic Times 34
Chapter 7   The Engine That Drove the Cotton Industry....40
Chapter 8   The Devil We Didn't Know 49
Chapter 9   They Chose Salvation 54
Chapter 10 Finding Courage..59
Chapter 11 I Have Decided..65
Chapter 12 It's Time to Go 67
Chapter 13 A New Beginning—In the Army Now 77
Chapter 14 Becoming a WAC...84
Chapter 15 One Week to Go—Graduation........................92

Acknowledgments 95
Glossary 97
About the Author 105

Introduction

●●●

Look! I Can Fly is part I of my autobiography, and it's an introduction to my early life. A life filled with hardship, poverty, disappointment, uncertainty, violence and fear. This book tells how these circumstances, fueled with other traumatic events, left a visible imprint on my life. Part 1 of my story, begins at three years old, and continues through the age of eighteen. As I retell my story, each of the coming chapters breathe life into the hopes and dreams of a little Black girl growing up in the rural Mississippi Delta, during the time of the Civil Rights Movement and the Vietnam War.

My story, offers unique insight into a nation in chaos, and divided over the Civil Rights Movement and the Vietnam War. At that time, both events were at its pinnacle, and not everyone supported the causes. Some who didn't agree, took to the streets in protest. While some others, donned disguises and wreaked havoc on a segment of society and their supporters. This story also tells of my personal struggles with domestic violence and bullying. And, how these acts of violence, and that of the Civil Rights Movement darken my spirit.

In addition, part 1 of my autobiography provides a brief genealogical overview of my family's lineage. A look back at how it all began for my family, and how being born of a certain race, or ethnic background determined the fate of my life. Also, this book offers a glimpse into the lives of the poor, uneducated laborers who lived and worked on the cotton farms in the Mississippi Delta.

But through it all, I found hope, courage, and learned how to persevere during the tough times, and then, navigate through the minefields and pitfalls of life. The spirit of hope helped me develop the tools needed to step out from the shadow of my painful circumstances, and take a giant leap of faith.

Get comfortable, and get ready to take a riveting, spine-tingling, and thought-provoking adventure into the early life of Dakota J. Land.

Chapter 1

In the Beginning

I was born in poverty to a teenage mother, and a father twenty years older than her. My mother, the daughter of a sharecropper, was born in the State of Mississippi, on a farm called Woodburn Plantation, near the end of the Great Depression (1929–1939). Mom said, "There were so many Black people living there, we had our own school and a US Post Office." Her parents were married at the beginning of the depression, and they had seven children. Mom completed the eighth grade; and she could read and write. For which, she was very proud. This was a big deal for the time. Mom said, "Everyone worked in the fields, including small children. My older siblings didn't get much schooling, because they worked alongside Daddy, especially during, and immediately after the great depression."

One of my paternal grandmother's sisters was ninety-three when she told me about my paternal ancestors. She said, "Your father, grandparents and great-grandmother were born on a farm called the Enola Plantation, near the Yazoo River in Mississippi. Your paternal great-grandfather was born into slavery on or about 1847 in Alabama. His enslaver brought him and three sons, also born into slavery, to the Enola Plantation, sometime before the US Civil War (1861-1865). Our family continued to live and work, as farm laborers, on that land through the late 1930s."

My paternal grandfather was born in early 1880, and my paternal grandmother was born in early 1890s. They had eight children, my father being the youngest boy. He was born in the late 1900s, in Mississippi. He could not read or write, but he could identify and count money. His military enlistment papers indicate that he completed the sixth grade, but he claimed to have completed the second. Despite his inability to read or write, he served honorably in the US Army, during World War II.

I loved the art of reading, and books fed my growing curiosity and vivid imagination. I often transported myself into a story and traveled wherever the author wanted to go. My imagination kept my spirit of adventure alive, as well as, my desire to learn more about the world. Learning to read and write came easily to me. Rose, my oldest sister, was my first teacher. She was six and I was three. Rose was in the first grade, and when she did her homework, I was allowed to learn with her. When I colored outside the lines, she tapped my hand with her pencil, and would say, "No, don't do it that way." By the age of four, I could recite the alphabet and write the letters, and to everyone's surprise, I could read Rose's first grade reader. But Rose, became suspicious somehow, and gave me a spelling test, which I failed. I had memorized every word in the book based on the pictures on each page. After that big reveal, Mom worked with me while Rose was at school. Mom taught me how to sound the letters and spell words. She started with small words of things familiar to me like, cat, dog, rat, ball, broom and pig. By the time Rose moved to the third grade, I was reading at the second-grade level.

Two and a half months after celebrating my sixth birthday, I began first grade, which was exciting at first. But a few days into the school year, my peers began to taunt, tease, ridicule, and even hit me. I hadn't expected that, and I had no idea how to handle that awful situation.

To avoid being harassed in the classroom, I modeled the behavior of another student, who stuttered. My teacher didn't ask much of me, and determined that I best fit between the B and the D students. That placement worked great for me until my aunt, the other first grade teacher at my school, appeared in my classroom doorway. Later that morning, my teacher asked me to read. My performance was lackluster at best. My teacher said, "I know who you are. You are from teacher stock. You're going to read until I tell you to stop. If you don't, I'll whip you until you do."

I didn't believe her, and stuttered through a few more lines. She said, "Give me your hand," and she began to hit me with a leather strap. It hurt, and I cried, but she wouldn't stop hitting me. The other students in the classroom watched as the punishment transformed me from a stutterer to speaking and reading perfect English. When she was satisfied, she stopped hitting me, snatched the book, and told me to sit down. My sniffling continued long after the punishment stopped, because my aunt's betrayal had made me a bigger target for the classroom bullies.

Before class ended that day, my teacher said to me, "Gather your things and move to the A table." The students at the A table were the children of the Black community's most notable citizens: educators, insurance agents, landowners, and school administrators. The A table was the last place I wanted to be. *If only I could magically disappear. But, this wasn't a fairy tale, and I couldn't just disappear. But, Lord knows, I sure wanted to.* My fellow first-grade classmates hated me and wouldn't allow me to attend class in peace. That was how my academic life began.

Despite the troublesome start, my grades didn't suffer. After about two months, the first-grade teacher advanced the students at the A table, including me to the second grade. The second-grade teacher determined that the third grade would have been the appropriate grade for me, but Mom said, "No." She wrote a note to the teacher stating: "She's too young. The third-grade students would be too old, making it difficult for her to fit in." I was disappointed that she didn't say yes, because this plan would have allowed me to escape the bullying that had taken on a life of its own.

By the third grade, my grades began to slip and my interest in learning waned. My tormenters stole my joy, and I didn't like school anymore. I never understood why children who looked like me could be so mean. Their actions were cruel, and no child should have to endure such behavior. I suffered in silence because of fear, and that affected my self-esteem. People in authority should have known about the unhealthy behavior, but I didn't have the courage, or the confidence to tell them, and they didn't care enough about me to notice.

Bullying should never be hidden or tolerated in the classroom, playground, the workplace, home—anyplace. Bullying hurts people, and hurt people hurt others. Bullying has been outlawed and classified as a crime in most states in the United States. Despite this declaration, the crime of bullying continues.

We lived on a farm in a plain, old, wood-framed house with three small rooms. It sat off a dirt road past an old, two-story barn, and near a bayou. It was surrounded on three sides by miles of cotton fields. A huge, old pecan tree in the backyard offered shade in the summer, and delicious pecans in the fall. Also, there was a big pear tree a few yards farther from the back of the house. It produced sweet juicy pears for many years.

Despite how much I hated that old house, Mom said to me one day, "Most of y'all were born right here in this house. And, y'all were delivered by mid-wives." Of course, I asked, "What's a mid-wife?" Her response didn't make sense to me at the time. However, one of my brothers disputed the claim of being delivered by a mid-wife, because the White doctor signed his birth certificate. Mom had an answer for that too. She said, "A few days after a home birth, the mother and baby would go for a checkup with the White doctor, it was at that point, the application for a birth certificate was filed, and the physician would sign the document. Mom said, "Poor Black families, like ours, couldn't afford the expense of a professional practitioner to deliver a baby."

When I was little, I remember my paternal grandmother being present every time one of my younger siblings were born. And, I remember her, introducing us to a new sister or brother, saying, "Look what the stork delivered." My paternal grandmother worked like a superhero, and made multitasking look easy. She cooked, took care of Mom, the baby, the house, and my siblings and me. She stayed busy, as she hummed an old church hymn, and she dared us children to be disobedient. Even Dad acted like a little boy around her. He didn't cuss, or fuss at Mom, or us when Grandma was there. She was mean, but I wished she would have stayed at our house, because she brought calm to an otherwise chaotic living environment, ripe with fear and violence. The time she spent with us was invaluable to me.

Our family continued to grow, but its economic health didn't keep pace with the times. Mom handmade clothes for my sisters and me. Sometimes, she was able to purchase fabric, and other times, she used material from hand-me-down dresses given to her to wear, but instead, she took the dresses apart, and made little matching outfits for my sisters and me. Her creations were beautiful in my eyes, but my peers made jokes about me at school, because my clothes were not like theirs - store-bought.

Mom sacrificed her appearance for us, and I never forgot that. As I matured into a young adult, buying new clothes for Mom became a priority for me. As my finances increased, my gifts to her became more extravagant. If a size was off, she loved it anyway. Mom's first new coat, was sent to her from the Sears and Roebuck Catalogue. The sleeves were too short, but she didn't care, and wore it anyway. She refused to return it for fear it would get lost. While she lived, I wanted her to know that I appreciated everything she did for my siblings and me.

Chapter 2

The Perils of Living on a Farm

Growing up on a farm offered open space, fresh air, fun, adventure, and elements of great risk. Danger lurked in the shadows of every weed, bush, log, the shores of the bayou, and the barn. Sometimes a reptile would slither from the bayou to the insides of the house, or take refuge in our play areas. If we ventured too close, it would strike. Bees and wasps are good for the environment, but can be harmful to humans. One day my brother Jack disturbed a beehive, and we all were stung, but he got it the worst. His head swelled so big, it looked like a giant jack-o-lantern No one knew that he was allergic to bee stings. He was lucky, our parents were home, and they rushed him to the doctor. Despite our parents' good intentions, Mother Nature was out of their control.

Sometimes, danger could be avoided, but other times it could not. It was the twilight of the evening, and I said, "Goodbye to another sweltering summer day." I found a quiet corner inside the house, and became engrossed in the suspense and intrigue of a new book. I hadn't noticed how dark my surroundings had become. Surprised by the lateness, I hurried outside to take in the laundry that had been drying for hours in the hot afternoon sun. As I walked toward the big pecan tree in the backyard, a cool breeze brushed my cheeks, *the breath of an angel, so soothing, gentle, and refreshing.* The breeze cooled the moisture that had formed on my skin due to the high humidity. I slowed my pace to fully enjoy the moment. During the summer in southeastern part of the United States, the days were long, hot, and humid, and the nights were not much cooler. *Oh, how I wished we had one of those new cooling devices, called an air conditioner. A luxury item, and too expensive for a poor family like ours.* We had one fan, and the family gathered close by it to keep cool. Sometimes, Mom would sit the fan in the window to try and capture a cooler breeze, but when the temperature reached a hundred, the fan simply recirculated the hot air.

As darkness covered the landscape. The crickets chirped, lightning bugs danced in the distance, bullfrogs croaked and ribbited, as the chickens and pigeons sheltered for the night. The pigs were quite too. The big pecan tree loomed over the backyard, and it cast an extra layer of darkness over the area. The butterflies in my stomach took flight and reminded me that the backyard was no place to be after dark. I tried to refocus on the chore, and quickly removed laundry from the line with my right hand, and placed it on my left arm. The fresh crisp scent usually relaxed me, but that night, it provided no comfort. The weight of the laundry on my arm had become uncomfortable, as it was stacked up to my chin. I wanted to remove it all, at one time, to avoid having to comeback outside in the dark. As I adjusted the bundle in my arm, I felt a scratch on my right foot, but attributed it to thorns on a blackberry vine. To avoid the hazard, I looked down. Horrified, I dropped the big bundle of laundry, screamed as loud as possible, and ran through the darkness, as fast as I could, screaming, "Mom, Mom, Mom."

Time slowed down, the front door appeared to move farther and farther away. But, just as I landed on the front porch, Jack opened the door, and I ran through it. He asked, "What's wrong with you?" I didn't respond. Mom was sitting on the bed with a bowl of popcorn, with the look of wonderment in her eyes as I approached her. I thrusted my foot in her face, and the popcorn spilled on the bed and floor. I said, "Mom, something bit me."

When I opened my eyes, all of my siblings were standing over me, and talking all at once. There was sadness in Mom's eyes, and her voice lacked its usual vitality and enthusiasm. It was what I didn't see in Mom's eyes, that scared me. Images of what had happened in the backyard flooded my mind. My body warmed up, and the awful feeling in my stomach, made me nauseated. *Was this a dream or a nightmare? Did I get bitten by two snakes? Why me?* I finally summoned the courage to look at my foot, but half of it had been neatly wrapped with a homemade bandage – *Mom's handiwork.* She had no formal education beyond eighth grade, but she studied books on how to properly use herbs and over-the-counter medications to treat wounds, and other minor illness.

I asked, "Mom, am I going to die?"

"It's in God's hands," she said.

What could I do, besides wait to die? The thought of dying ruined the serenity of the early evening, and darken the spirit that had come so freely in the warm summer night.

Jack said, "Your screams scared us and interrupted the TV show we were watching. We spilled our popcorn too. Your screams woke up the chickens, and hurt my ears. Why didn't you just come through the back door? It was closer."

Inside my head, I was screaming - Mom, please make him stop talking. Why's he talking so much? I was too exhausted to answer his questions. "Mom, please help me, tell him to stop bothering me. He's working my nerves," I whispered. This was Jack, the first boy, and he had to be in the mix of everything.

Mom's youngest brother stopped by unexpectedly, and she told him about the incident. It was a Saturday night, and Dad had already left for the evening. After hearing the story, He said, "I will go find Hank, and bring him back." Not long after, they returned, and Dad asked me, "What happened?" I didn't want to remember, or tell what I had seen. I hated snakes. I wished that he would just go look where I had left the laundry, but he didn't. He waited for a response from me. My heart was racing, when I said, "I think two snakes bit me. Because, I saw the heads of two snakes go under that big log in the backyard."

Dad didn't scare easily, but for a moment, he looked scared. Jack told Dad his version of what had happened, even though he hadn't been with me outside. Then he told Dad about what he saw Mom do to my foot. Dad asked our uncle to go outside with him to look for the snakes. He used the lights on his work tractor to light up the backyard, where the bundle of dry laundry still lay.

As we watched from the windows, they carefully lifted the laundry piece by piece. Because Mom said to them, "Y'all better not bring no snakes back into the house." She was afraid of them too. Then they moved the log, Dad said in a loud excited voice, "Expletive, it's two of them." After the reptiles were neutralized, Dad and uncle each held one up high, and called me to come take a look. I refused to go back out there. From the window, I saw two snakes, a big, long one, and another, about half the size of the first. Dad later said, "They were dry land moccasins—a mother and baby that had taken refuge under the log, which had been left after a construction project near the house." Then Dad said to Mom, "Your quick thinking may have saved her life."

Dad said to me, "I wanted you to see that the snakes couldn't hurt you anymore." He was wrong. The incident forever etched in my memory, and the thought of what happened, gave me chills, and nightmares. I wanted to forget, but my mind wouldn't cooperate.

Chapter 3

Saved by Grace

According to at least one expert, it was a miracle that I hadn't died. After a prolonged illness, at the age of five, the small-town doctor said to my parents, "I can't do anything else for her. Take her home, make her comfortable, and she'll naturally recover or pass on." I didn't understand what he meant. Dad looked dejected and gloomy. Mom's beautiful face looked like all its muscles had disappeared. She looked sullen. On the long ride home, they didn't talk to each other, or to me. When it was time for bed, Mom did as the doctor had suggested. She placed me in a chair and stuffed pillows around me to prevent me from falling forward during the night.

Usually, when I was sick, Mom was very attentive, but that time, she was different. She left me alone, and Dad didn't check on me either.

Sometime during the night, the angel of death beckoned

me. A warm, yellowish glow at the end of a long, narrow bridge drew me closer. A voice said, "Go back. It's not your time."

"No, I'm coming."

The bridge, suspended high above a lush, green valley with a narrow waterway snaking through it, ended in front of the yellowish glow. Behind the large circle of yellow was a wide wall of white light that opened into infinity. Halfway across the bridge, the warm, yellowish glow began to radiate like the sun. Its presence was strong and continued to pull me forward. My spirit wanted to be one with it. The yellow glow comforted me, and I was not afraid. Unlike the time I followed Mom across the Dawson Lake Bridge. The space between the planks on the bridge were wide enough to see the glistening water below, and I struggled to keep my tiny feet from getting stuck in the openings. As a four-year-old child, I feared the cracks would open wider, and I would fall into the water.

My date with death was close, my journey across the long bridge was almost complete. The voice spoke again, and this time the tone was different, more urgent, but yet caring and calm. It said, "Turn around now. Go back. Don't look down, because you will be afraid." Again, I heard, "It's not your time." I didn't want to turn around, but something stronger than my own will took control of my body, and turned me around on that narrow bridge.

I woke up to the brightest sunlight smiling through my window. Mom was up early that morning also. I watched as she quietly open the door to my room and eased her head around it. *What's she doing? Playing a game?* I couldn't wait to tell her about my experience the night before. Excited, I said "Mom, God talked to me last night. Mom, I talked to God." Mom rushed into the room, and removed the pillows that had held me in the chair.

Excited, I almost leaped out of the chair, "Mom, I was walking across a long bridge, and God was talking to me. His voice was coming from behind a big yellow glowing light. Mom, it was real. It was so beautiful."

"Hush, hush, hush your mouth, girl."

We didn't know it at the time, but I had been saved by God's grace. Hence, a miracle had occurred. The childhood illness would never come again. It wasn't long after that experience that Mom sought salvation and was water baptized.

God's Angels continued to watch over us. Because on one of the hottest days of the summer, Jack set fire to dry grass in the backyard near one of the outbuildings. I was six, and he was five. He said, "I'm going to bake me a potato for lunch."

Dad had built a shed over an underground storage area. He stored potatoes and similar food items there covered with straw to preserve for use later. Jack took a box of matches, and headed to the storage area. Rose, our oldest sister, had been left to supervise us, but she couldn't keep an eye on Jack and me, and a child under two. When she saw Jack with the matches, she told him, "Put those matches down." But Rose was just nine, and we didn't respect her authority.

The straw was dry and packed tight. Jack struck a match and dropped it. The fire started slow, Jack tried to stomp it out, but that made the fire become bigger. Then, I stomped and fanned it with my hands, but it got bigger, and started moving toward the house. "Rose, come help us," I yelled. She stood in the kitchen with the baby on her hip, and watched us from the back door. "Y'all better come from out there," she screamed. At that point, the fire was as tall as the shed.

Dad appeared out of nowhere, huffing and puffing, and Mom was a few minutes behind him. As Jack and I stood there in shock, Dad snatched Jack from the path of the inferno, and disappeared. When he returned he had a bucket of water in each hand, and threw it on the raging fire. After a few more bucket of water, he brought the fire under control. I couldn't believe the speed at which Dad moved. Blinded by the smoke, fire, and fear, I didn't see where he had gotten the water to stop that wild monster that Jack created.

Superman had nothing on Dad that day. I was beyond happy that he and Mom had been working in a nearby field, and could see the house. Mom said, "From what we could see, we thought the house was on fire."

Mom asked Rose, "What happened?"

"I saw Jack with the matches," she said, "but I don't know who started the fire. They both were out there."

Mom turned to me, and I said, "Jack did it. I tried to stop him, but he wouldn't listen." Before she could questioned Jack, he said "I didn't do it, she did it," pointing at me.

Mom had already selected a nice thin switch from the cotton field to execute the punishment. The thin switches hurt the worst, and I was happy that she started with the little liar first. She gave him a few swats on the butt, he screamed, squirmed, and tried to run away. Then water began to saturate the front of his pants. I slapped both hands over my mouth to hide the shock, and surprise of what I was seeing. If Mom had seen my reaction, she would have given me a double helping for laughing at Jack's situation. When she finished with him, I started crying before she got to me.

"Why are you crying?" she asked me. "I haven't touched you yet."

"Because I didn't do nothing."

She hit me one time with the switch, and I collapsed crying and hollering as loud as I could. Jack was the only boy, and all of the adults loved him, and spoiled him rotten. In my opinion, little brothers were nothing but trouble. Jack got away with all sorts of things because he was a beautiful boy. I wanted to return Jack to the stork farm. Because, he always got me into trouble. Corporal punishment was an approved method for correcting a child's behavior in decades past. I think it helped Jack, because he never started a fire again.

As life would have it, this was not the end of this story. For more than thirty years, the truth about who set the fire, remained a point of contention between Jack and me. Some family members believed his version of the story, and others mind. I was surprised that the lie had continued for such a long time, and had not been resolved. I remembered hearing that if you can tell the same lie, the same way, over and over again, it becomes the truth. This lie had continued for so long, I was ready to accept it as the truth, and move on.

As fate would have it, at a family gathering, someone brought up the story about the fire. Out of the blue, Jack said, "I did it."

I asked him, "You did what?"

"I started the fire in the backyard that summer long ago," he said.

"What?" I asked again.

"You heard me. I did it," he said.

His confession took me by surprise, and it shocked me. I couldn't believe what I had heard. But no one else appeared to care. This lack of interest shocked me too, because over the years, many of these relatives had sided with Jack.

"Why tell the truth now?" I asked.

"I found Jesus," he said, "and I want to go to heaven."

I shook my head in disbelief, but I was happy that the hope of salvation inspired him to confess the truth.

For us, life was never like a bowl of cherries. When I was eight a sudden and violent storm formed over our little farmhouse. The storm brought high winds, heavy rain, pounding thunder, and crackling lightning that made us fear for our lives. We ran to Mom for comfort and protection. A big gust of wind forced opened the front door, and it hit the floor with a bang. Mom looked in the direction of the door; her eyes wide, as if she had seen a ghost. The house shook, the windows rattled, and the glass cracked. Fear and danger, battled each other on the porch, like the ancient gods of Olympias, to see who would be first to enter the house. They moved about like giant wrestlers. They grunted, stomped, pushed and shoved each other, and clang their long shiny swords, as gigantic bolts of lightning flashed, and the boom from the thunder shook the house. The noise was louder than anything that I had ever heard. My siblings and I were afraid, and we clung to the side of the bed where Mom laid. Fear won the battle, and as he stepped over the threshold.

Mom screamed, "Run. Hide in the closet."

"Come with us," I said.

Mom couldn't run because she was in a full body cast. She had been seriously injured in an episode of domestic violence about a year earlier, and she was trapped in her bed. She couldn't move, and we were too small to help her. With the same force that fear and danger used to force open the front door, they drove debris and rain into the house with the same strength. Mom was helpless and exposed to the danger.

As Rose hurried us to the closet, I looked back, and saw Mom cover her head with the bedding. The closet was small but large enough that day to provide safety and protection for us kids. Rose, then eleven, held the two-year-old perched on her hip, while my four siblings huddled together in fear. I stood alone, trembling and crying, because Mom was alone. The closet was dark and hot, and the noise caused by the storm was loud and frightening. Heavy sheets of rain poured down on the tin roof, lighting crackled, thunder boomed and grumbled, and the tin used to cover the roof flapped, and made a weird tapping sound, as the wind swooshed and whistled.

We cowered in the closet as the storm continued to terrorize us. We heard Mom moaning, praying, and occasionally

screaming. It sounded like she was being tortured. I peeked through tiny cracks in the closet wall hoping to see her, but couldn't, because the cracks didn't open into her room. I cried louder, hoping that my wailing would cancel out the noise of the storm. But my crying had no effect. The storm was too powerful.

After a while, the noise quieted down and the storm moved away. We exited the closet and moved with caution around the broken glass, sticks, the down door, water and mud to get to mom. She was alive, but she was shaking as if she had a bad chill. The bed and everything on it, including Mom were soaked. Even her hair was wet, and the water dripped down her face like she had been washing it. The bed and Mom were covered with mud, sticks, and glass. Mom rubbed my face because I was still crying. "Go find dry clothes or bedding," she said, "and bring it back to me."

Eager to help her, we ran off to search for anything dry. This turned out to be a difficult task, because almost everything inside the house was wet, or had blown outside, and now rested in pools of water and mud. We rushed back to Mom with the few dry things we could find, and did our best to help her.

We heard a noise in the distance, and knew it was Dad coming home. The unique clicking noise that the engine of his old tractor made, always got our attention. He was driving slow, which made me think that he didn't know what had happened to us.

Look! I Can Fly

I said, "He must not know what happened?" Then, all of us kids went out to the porch, and jumped up and down, as we called him, "Daddy. Daddy." He must have heard us because he increased his sped a bit, and was soon in the house. He observed the damage, and tried to calm us. Because we were all talking at once. He checked each of us to make sure that we were okay. Then he attended to Mom.

"I got struck by lightning," Mom whispered to him.

"What?"

He stood still for what looked like forever before he continued to remove the wet bedding from around her. He then swept up the debris and mopped up the water on the floor. He rehung the front door and put temporary coverings over the windows. The tin roof was damaged too, but he said, "The rain had passed and this repair could have to wait for another day."

The next day, we surveyed the damage outside. The state-of-the-art chicken hotel that Dad built was destroyed. It had collapsed. The chickens looked lost wondering around the yard that morning. We found some of our clothes and other household items outside in the mud and water. The outhouse suffered damage too. It now leaned to one side. A few limbs from the old pecan tree rested on the ground waiting to become firewood.

The most startling thing of all, the big old pear tree, had been struck by lightning, and it was split straight down the middle. Now, it was a new tree with two arms, one pointing north and the other south. The trauma didn't kill it, but it never bore fruit again. With its battle scars evident for all to see, it stood proudly like a monument to a great war noting that something important had happened at this location.

"When's that old tree going to die?" Visitors would ask.

"Only Mother Nature knows," Mom would say.

For years, that old pear tree served as a reminder of the wrath of Mother Nature. It also reflected other powerful lessons about life. For example, how at a moment's notice an individual's life could be changed. Yesterday, your path took you in one direction, but today, it might lead you in another. The old pear tree, despite its injury, stood proud with its new look, and continued to live, and spark curiosity, until man decided to remove it from existence.

Chapter 4

Unaccompanied Minors

During the summer, Rose and I took unaccompanied trips on a Greyhound bus to visit our aunts and uncles who lived about thirty miles away. On our first trip, Rose was eight and I was five. Dressed in our best Sunday dresses, shoes, and socks and with cloth ribbons tied on our pigtails, we departed for the bus station with Mom.

As the passengers boarded the bus, I noticed the Black passengers going to the back of the bus, and the White passengers took seats in the front and the middle section of the bus. We were at the end of the line and Mom pushed us forward. I looked back and saw tears running down her face. "Mommy, aren't you coming with us?" I asked. She didn't respond. I noticed that she was looking at the bus driver, and he was looking at us. Mom made eye contact with him, which was unusual at that time. *Her eyes said, Mister, please take my children safely to their destination.*

At first, the driver looked mean. His stare was cold, and he didn't even blink. His forehead was all wrinkled up, but then he became more relaxed. Mom lifted me to the first step of the bus, while Rose boarded unassisted. The bus driver took our tickets and said, "Sit over there," pointing to two seats right behind him. During the trip, the driver didn't speak to us, but he watched us in his rearview mirror. I wanted to stick out my tongue at him, and put my fingers in my ears to make elephant ears to taunt him, but Mom had warned me not to be bad because the driver might put us off the bus.

When we arrived at our destination, he said, "This is your stop." Then he exited the bus and opened the compartment that contained the passengers' luggage. Rose and I didn't have a suitcase, and I wondered why Mom didn't have one for us. From the window near where Rose sat, I saw Aunt Virginia, Uncle Richard, and some of their children waiting for us outside the bus station. "The trip was long and boring," I told them.

The next summer's trip was mostly a repeat of the first. The driver seemed surprised to see us. Once again, we were the last to board. That time, the bus was almost full. He reached for our tickets and looked around to see where he could seat us. He asked a man sitting alone in the first seats to his left to take another seat. He told Rose and me, "Sit there."

We waved bye to Mom, who was crying. The big bus roared down the highway, but stopped on the side of the road a short time later. The driver opened the door and stood. I popped up like a jack-in-the-box. The driver looked at me, and said, "Sit down. This is not your stop." At the same time, Rose tugged on my arm. With a shrug of the shoulders, I exhaled a deep sigh, and said, "I just wanted to see what was happening."

Rose may have thought that I was about to get off the bus as I had when we rode the school bus home. The school bus stopped in front of our maternal grandfather's house, and I would sometime get off the bus, without telling anyone. The first time I did it, grandpa was surprised to see me, and asked me, "Do your parents know where you are?"

"No."

He offered me some food and then took me home.

Mom asked, "Why did you get off the bus at your grandpa's house?"

"I wanted to see him."

"How did you know he was home?"

"The door was open, and I saw the TV on."

The next time I surprised him, he smiled and didn't rush to take me home. We talked about school, watched TV, and ate some food that had been cooked for him. Later, Dad came to take me home.

Dad said to Grandfather, "We don't know what gets into that girl."

Grandpa said, "It's okay for her to come by."

My impromptu visits with Grandpa continued. He died the following year a few months before my birthday. Mom took it hard; she couldn't believe he had died. Afterwards, his wife moved away, and the door to his old house never open again. The school bus continued to stop there, to pick up children that lived nearby. Seeing his old house every day from the window of the school bus brought back memories of how much I enjoyed spending time with him, and it made me sad.

As the Greyhound bus sat on the side of the road, I tried my best to see what was happening. But, my view was blocked by Rose. Since the driver had scolded me, I didn't dare stand again. The wait was over, a thin, nice dressed, Black man boarded the bus, and strolled to the back to find a seat. The driver returned, took his seat, and our journey resumed. My mind was filled with questions. *Why didn't he get on the bus at bus station? Who was he? Who left him on the side of the road? And, where was he going?*

When we arrived at our destination, the driver stood, looked at me, and said, "Now you can get up. This is your stop." I knew where we were, because I could see our aunt and uncle. They were there waiting for us. The driver made me mad, and in my head, I stuck my tongue out at him in defiance. Mom always made me promise to be good, and if she or my aunt knew what I was thinking, they would put a belt to my backside. So, I kept my thoughts about the driver to myself.

I couldn't wait to tell Uncle Richard about what had happened on the trip. Uncle Richard said, "It's common for the Greyhound bus to stop if someone flagged it down, or if the driver sees someone with a suitcase on the side of the road." I asked him, "Why?" He said, "That's just how it is."

Rose and my summer travel routine continued until we were teenagers. The driver was the same on that route for all the years that we traveled unaccompanied. When we reached our teen years, we boarded the bus without Mom in attendance, and picked our own seats. We avoided the seats near the driver, even if the seats were open. Because I associated those seats with being a little child that the driver had to watch. Regardless of the seats we chose, the driver continued to look out for us. During our trips, he would scan the passengers from his rearview mirror, until he spotted Rose and me. I pretended not to see him looking for us, as I secretively watched him.

The driver showed kindness and professionalism to two little Black girls and their mother, during a time when racial tensions were high in the South. Knowing what I know now, and considering the time period, he could have refused to transport, us, unaccompanied minors in the 1960s, without any consequence. If he were alive at the time of this writing, he would be well over a hundred.

Those bus trips inspired my spirit of adventure and endless imagination for travel, far beyond where a Greyhound bus could take me. Later, Mom experienced her own adventures on a Greyhound bus. She traveled from the State of Mississippi to Tulsa, Oklahoma to visit Rose at the birth of her first granddaughter; then to Chicago, Illinois to see her family; and to California to visit me. Afraid to fly, she chose the Greyhound bus as her mode of transportation to fulfill her spirit of adventure.

Chapter 5

When Weather Becomes a Foe

On a quiet Sunday afternoon, in late February, 1971, a large tornado roared through our small southern town. It killed many residents that day, and destroyed or damaged schools, homes, and businesses. It brought winds of more than 261 miles per hour, and was later classified as an F-5 tornado, one of the strongest ever recorded, and it wasn't in Kansas.

I was fourteen at the time, and was alone babysitting two younger cousins. Their parents and my oldest sister returned home minutes before the massive tornado struck. I heard a loud rumbling noise that sounded like a train. I headed outside to watch it pass, but Rose grabbed me by the arm and pulled me back to the sofa. Confused by her actions, I was about to ask her why she had done that, but the house started shaking, and the rumbling got louder. Thomas, my cousin's husband, said, "Get into the bathtub!" As if he knew what was coming. Then he ran off to get the two children, who were sleeping in another room.

Rose and I sat in the bathtub and held onto the two children. My cousin crouched on the floor between the bathtub and the sink, and Thomas held onto the sink as the house swayed from side to side. It sounded like two locomotives were trying to get inside.

The house made weird noises: it grunted, moaned, cried, and wailed until every nail, bolt, and screw had released its grip on the structure. The house lifted off its foundation and swayed in the wind like a feather. I looked up and saw the roof seemingly inhaled and exhaled, and then it flew off toward the heavens. The walls collapsed outward. The window panes cracked and some burst out. Only a section of the bathroom where we had taken shelter was intact. The wind gently settled that section in the backyard. It took only a few minutes for the massive storm to destroy families, homes, businesses, schools, and the financial well-being of many. My spirit was numb, I didn't know what to do, think or how to feel, at that moment.

Thomas, who appeared composed, led us through the rubble and the debris to the street. My shoes had blown away along with their furniture and other household items. I sustained minor cuts and splinters to my feet, because I had to walk without shoes. My cousin's house had been destroyed with us in it. Their car was still parked on the street, where the front of their house once stood. The car was not damaged. And thank goodness, Thomas had keys to the car in his pocket. Many of the neighbors cars had been flipped over, and tossed into the nearby field. The street looked like a war zone. The house next to theirs had exploded, and the only things left of it, were the

concrete foundation and the chimney. I learned that the family who lived in that house had left on vacation a few days earlier.

Lifeless bodies rested in trees like rag dolls. The living were traumatized, and they moved about like zombies, as the daylight faded, and the night eagerly covered all that had been lost.

Looking across the railroad tracks, the scene at the elementary school, took my breath away, the school had sustained serious damage. The wing closest to the railroad tracks had been sheared off. When I attended that school, the damaged section would have housed the first through fifth grade classrooms. If the tornado had hit on a weekday, those classrooms would have been occupied. That would have increased the likelihood that the injury and loss of life would have been much larger, and more traumatic.

That day, the people most affected by the tornado had no warning of its approach and potential catastrophic damage. State-of-the-art weather technology had not been developed in the early 1970s. People in the impacted areas did their usual Sunday activities. The church people went to church, mothers prepared meals, children played outside, and sinners sinned.

As soon as the tornado had moved away, cousin Thomas took us to the hospital. And from there, we went to our house. At that time, Mom and Dad were living apart. We walked in the front door. Everyone stood and stared at us. Mom's eyes rolled back in her head, and she collapsed.

"What's wrong with Momma?" I asked.

Cousins Roberta and Thomas rushed to her, and offered aid. Jack said that Dad had just left after telling Mom, "A big tornado struck the town a few miles away. Dakota, Rose, Thomas, Roberta, and the kids were all dead. Everything was destroyed. No one could have survived. I'm going back to look for the bodies. And, I told you to stop allowing Dakota and Rose spend so much time away from home." Jack said, "The news upset Mom."

A few days later, I saw Dad, and asked him, "How did he know about the tornado, and how did he get to Mom's house so fast?" He said, "I was already in town, at Millie's place, when a man came to the door and yelled, 'A tornado just hit the south side of town.' I knew you and Rose were there, so I went to see if I could help, and check on y'all. Not finding y'all and seeing how badly the area had been hit, I figured that y'all must have died, and your bodies had blown away, and that, I had to tell your mother before she heard it on the news, or from someone else."

Mom and Dad had been separated for a few months, at that time, due to decades of physical and emotional abuse. My siblings and I lived with Mom. She found a small, run-down house facing a busy street within walking distance to the elementary, junior and senior high schools. The house had working indoor plumbing, a big step up from what we had left behind. Dad remained on the farm alone in his house.

Those were the best, and the worst times in my life. It was the best of times, because Dad was not living in our house. It was the worst of times because Mom was sad, and very pregnant. Regardless, I prayed for them to never reconcile. She had left before, but she had always returned whenever, he would come calling with hat in hand. Mom probably thought her love would make him a better man, but it didn't. She couldn't fix what was broken in my father, and he wasn't willing, or able to fix himself. I wondered if he had been like that before the war, or if something had happened to him during World War II. He had a hair-trigger temper, and he directed all that violence toward Mom. Living with him was like being trapped in a tiny cave with a huge, angry, one-eyed monster whose urge to fight was never satisfied.

The absence of violence, and related chaos in our home allowed me to focus on my studies, and I made the honor roll for the first time in tenth grade.

Chapter 6

Turbulent Social and Economic Times

I grew up during the mid-1960s and the early 1970s, the height of the Civil Rights Movement (1954–1968) and the Vietnam War (1955–1975). Through nonviolent protests, the Movement led to the Civil Rights Act of 1964, legislation that ended segregation in public places and banned employment discrimination on the basis of race, color, religion, sex or national origin. The Movement shed light on the inequity in education, voting rights, poverty, and living and working conditions for the poor, and people of color. Improvement in these areas would have significantly change the lives of people like me and my family. We lived below the federal poverty line, because my parents didn't earn a living wage. To complicate matters, my father had vices—gambling, drinking, and womanizing, which contributed to our predicament.

Our small house was not the best place to raise a family with children. The electricity was poorly wired. I feared that one day, the house would burn down. It didn't have indoor plumbing, and it was near a stagnant bayou, a perfect breeding grounds for mosquitos and reptiles. A big cow pasture across the road, in front of our house, offered its own hazardous conditions. The smell was awful, and the heat made it worse. The cows were huge and they often escaped from the pasture, and walk straight to the grounds surrounding our house. I hid for hours from the cows for fear they would hurt me. One time, I stayed hidden past the dinner hour, and Dad had to come shoo a cow away, and escort me to the house.

During the Civil Rights Era, violence against Blacks and the people who supported civil and equal rights were common. It was the worst of times for people of color. During my adolescent and early teenage years, assassins took the life of several notable political and civil rights leaders.

- Medgar Evers of Jackson, Mississippi, in 1963
- John F. Kennedy, president of the United States, in 1963
- Senator Robert F. Kennedy in 1968
- Dr. Martin Luther King Jr. in 1968

These brazen killings instilled fear and insecurity. Attending school, traveling on the school bus, going to church, and even being home made me feel unsafe. And, an easy target for people who didn't want to see fair and equal rights in the United States. I lived with the fear that they would kill me and my family. The following tragic events are etched in my memory.

Medgar Evers was gunned down in his driveway in Jackson, Mississippi on June 12, 1963, three days after my eighth birthday.

I was eight and in the fourth grade when an assassin took the life of President John F. Kennedy in Dallas, Texas on November 22, 1963. It was the last day of school before the Thanksgiving break. My classmates and I were playing in the hallway outside our classroom when my teacher ran down the hall crying and shouting, "They killed him. They killed the president."

In the excitement, I made an awkward move and stabbed myself in the thigh with a sharp pencil. It hurt, and I started to cry, which got my teacher's attention. In between her tears, she asked, "Why are you crying?"

"I stuck myself with a pencil."

I lifted my skirt to show her. The lead from the pencil had broken off and was lodged beneath my skin. The teacher used her fingernails to remove the lead. It left a scar that's visible to this day, and it's a reminder of that awful event.

The heinous murder of President Kennedy awakened the conscience of the nation. The majority of citizens stood up against hate, which moved forward the Voting Rights Act, a major piece of legislation that supported the Civil Rights Movement. On August 6, 1965, President Lyndon Johnson signed the act into law. It didn't change the hearts and minds of everyone, but it was a step in the right direction.

On April 4, 1968, Dr. Martin Luther King Jr. was assassinated in Memphis, Tennessee. I was twelve and in the seventh grade. Fear was thick in the air, and I was afraid to get on the school bus that afternoon. *Was this the day that all Black people would be* killed? Who would speak for us, and who would lead us now? Everyone who could have helped us and the Movement had been killed.

"Why are they killing us?" I asked Mom.

She just shook her head. Speechless.

Presidential candidate and US Senator Robert F. Kennedy was assassinated in Los Angeles, California on June 6, 1968, three days before my thirteenth birthday. We lived in fear, not knowing who would be next. I had become numb to the violence.

I asked my parents, "Why don't we leave this place?"

"And go where?" Mom asked.

"Anywhere but here."

"No place is perfect," she said. "You have to make your own way wherever you live."

One day during a voter registration drive, the landowner came to that little shack he provided for us, rested his feet on the porch, and called out, "Pearl, come out here. I want to talk to you."

"Yes sir," Mom said.

"I don't want you talking to those troublemakers coming around here trying to get you all to register to vote. Because that's White people's business."

"Yes sir," she said.

"You understand me?"

"Yes sir."

I was at her elbow when this conversation occurred. Her demeanor—watery eyes, shaky but soft voice, and arms folded tight over her chest—indicated to me that something about what he was saying bothered her. He left, and she was unusually quiet and looked dazed for the remainder of the day. I was six, their conversation and the dynamics between them had me very confused. *Why didn't he want Mom to register to vote?* The answer was clear, but I was too young to understand what the landowner had done.

For as long as I can remember, Mom told me about Emmitt Till, the fourteen-year-old Black boy who was brutally murdered by White men in a small town in the Mississippi Delta. She said, "The boy was murdered two months after you were born, and it had everyone scared. It touched my heart deeply because there I was with a new baby, and this mother would never see her son alive again. If they were brave enough to do that to a child, they could do just about anything to us. That's why we have to be careful around them."

Emmitt Till's murder stayed fresh in her mind. She talked about it as if it was yesterday. Sometimes I forgot, and thought she was talking about a recent murder, since Blacks were an easy target for those who wished to do us harm.

Despite the Civil Rights Movement, change was not immediate or significant in the area that I lived. In 1972, farm laborers who chopped cotton were paid $13 a day. At first, that was thought to be a lot of money back then, until the private drivers, that transported the workers to the worksite, were paid. Then it became much less than $13 a day. The schools didn't integrate, though they were legally required to under Federal law. Whites built expensive private schools for their children, while Blacks continued to attend public schools. The signs designating Black and White in public facilities were removed, but the hearts of those who put up the signs, in the first place, didn't change. The poor continued to work on farms, and lived in substandard houses.

While in high school during the years 1971 and 1972, I worked as a maid and babysitter and earned $1.50 an hour at one job and $15 a week at another. My high school offered the boys a program on farming, and the girls a program that taught them how to sew, cook, clean, and basically make a happy home. I believe that this was an unconscious effort by the high school to provide a trained labor force for the agricultural industry and domestic workers. In a sense, it trained young people of color to follow in their parents' footsteps. This was not the path I had in mind for my future. When the electives were offered to me, I chose to learn how to type instead of taking the home economics class.

After I graduated from high school, I went to the unemployment office and applied for typing jobs. The woman who interviewed me said, "We don't have any jobs like that available, but we do have immediate openings for maids in private homes throughout the community."

I responded, "I type fifty words per minute, and I'd like to wait for something in my area of interest."

I waited, but the unemployment office did not provide feedback or show any interest regarding my application for a typing position.

Chapter 7

The Engine That Drove the Cotton Industry

Cheap labor provided by the poor, and people of color were the engine that made the cotton industry profitable. Mom worked as a laborer, and Dad operated and repaired equipment used to plant, cultivate, and harvest cotton. That was how they made a living, and they were expected to groom their children to follow in their footsteps. The landowner told Mom when he thought one of the children were tall or old enough to begin working in the fields. When he thought that the boys in the house were tall enough to learn how to drive a tractor, he informed Dad. When my brother Jack was told at age thirteen that it was time for him to start driving a tractor, he left home to avoid doing that kind of work, and to continue his education.

Cotton farming demanded a lot of time and attention. My parents worked in the field regardless of the heat and humidity, sometimes six days a week from sunup to sundown. Their wages never compensated them enough for the awful working conditions they endured. When the planting and cultivating seasons were completed, my father picked up his hoe and worked alongside Mom removing the weeds from around the cotton. This was called chopping cotton. The landowner walked behind the laborers and inspected their work. When he found cotton chopped down with the weeds, he lost his temper. He yelled expletives at the laborers and reminded them to chop down weeds, not cotton.

In his fields, Johnson grass grew taller than the cotton, and it was tough to cut down. Sometimes, the blade on the hoe broke off, because the stalks of Johnson grass were thick and dense. Mom said, "When you get to Johnson grass before it gets too big, that's when it's easiest to remove." In this case, she said, "The landowner waited too long to put choppers in that field because he was probably trying to save money."

When I hit Johnson grass with my hoe, it felt like I was hitting a small tree, and the hoe reverberated out of my hand. Every time I hit it, the same thing would happen. Finally, someone more experienced would come over to help me. One day, an old man saw me trying to cut down one of those small trees, and said, "Girl, you gon' break your wrist. Let me show you how to do it." Of course, he removed it and a few cotton stalks too. The men would swing at the Johnson grass like they were trying to hit a golf ball. Mom said, "It was normal for a few cotton plants to fall with Johnson grass," but the landowner didn't want to lose any. He acted as if a few plants lost during this phase made a big difference at the harvest. Mom said, "Don't pay him no mind. Just keep on going."

One day, Dad was plowing a field near our house. We watched him from the backyard as clouds of thick dust rose up and followed the tractor, as he drove up and down the field. When the rows ended, he turned the tractor around and repeated the same function time and time again. All of a sudden, Jack yelled, "Mom, look, Dad's dead." He had slumped over to one side in his seat, and the tractor had changed course and was heading across the field. We screamed and yelled from the backyard trying to get his attention. Mom screamed his name, but he didn't hear her. The landowner was sitting in his truck, watching Dad work. After he saw what was happening, he began running across the field chasing the tractor. He called Dad's name, and he was cussing. He was yelling, "Stop that tractor. You plowing up my cotton."

Once again, it was all about the dollar for him. He was hilarious, but I couldn't laugh, because Dad was in danger. The tractor continued under its own power, and was heading toward a deep drainage ditch. We continued waving our hands and calling out to him. The landowner continued to chase the slow-moving tractor, and cussing. I stopped screaming, covered my eyes, and waited for them to say that Dad, and the tractor had crashed into the ditch. But, a tragedy was averted that day. Mom said, "He straighten up, right before he got to the ditch, and stopped the tractor." I removed my hands from my eyes, and Dad was wiping his face with his shirt sleeve, and looking confused. We all exhaled. Mom said, "Thank God! He must have just fallen asleep."

When the landowner caught up to Dad, he was cussing up a storm and pointing to where Dad had traveled across the field, leaving a noticeable open space where he had plowed across row after, row of cotton. We all laughed. My brothers were rolling around in the dirt holding their stomachs as they laughed.

I said, "He's probably telling Dad that he has to pay for the damage."

Mom laughed. "You're probably right."

Dad never missed a day of work even when he was sick, or hungover. In that case, he had stayed out late the night before, and the night before that. When he returned home at the end of the day, I asked him, "Daddy, what happened to you out there?"

He grinned and said, "It was nothing."

I knew that wasn't true because Mom was not talking to him.

The laborers chopped cotton from late spring through midsummer. It was hard and tedious work. They walked row after row all day long in the heat, which could reached 100 degrees, and the humidity often reached 85 or 90 percent. The landowner provided ice water when large groups of people were hired, but when it was just my parents, they had to provide water for themselves. A brief break was allowed for lunch, which was taken in the field unless they were working nearby.

By midsummer, the cotton would be three to four feet tall and in some places taller, which made it difficult to see your feet. Snakes frequented the fields during this time, looking to cool off under the thick foliage. That was a hazard the workers had to look out for too. When the plants became too big to plow, or to chop, this was called the lay-by-season, which was between the cultivation and cotton-picking seasons.

During this time, Mom canned all kinds of vegetables, and preserved different kinds of fruits. Also, she led a quilting circle. Mom and several other women from the nearby farms would get together and make a quilt for each person in the group. They took this time to catch up on their girl talk. Sometimes these meetings got lively, because Mom would steal some of Dad's corn liquor, and shared it with the ladies. After one of those sessions, the patterns on the quilts didn't look so good. But that didn't matter to them. They would just laugh at their handiwork, and move on to the next one.

Prior to the invention of the mechanized cotton picker, laborers performed the backbreaking work of removing the cotton from the dried bolls by hand. The dried bolls contained sharp points like needles that pricked their fingers almost every time the cotton was removed. Pricks from the bolls irritated the fingers and hands, and cause inflammation and scarring. Some pickers used gloves or old socks to try to protect their hands. After removing the cotton from the bolls, the adult pickers used long, thick, cloth sacks attached over their shoulders that they dragged behind them to hold the cotton.

Mom worked hard, and she was a fast picker. She often stuffed more than 180 pounds of cotton in her sack. As she filled it, my siblings and I would sometimes ride on her sack while she filled it. Ten-or twelve-year-old children used something called a Croker sack, it was about a third the size of an adult sack, looped over their shoulders to hold the cotton they picked. As a child, I liked going to the cotton field with Mom, but picking cotton was hard, and my attention span was short. The people, the conversations, the songs, the birds, butterflies, worms, and the magic of the cotton itself kept me distracted.

The cotton pickers were paid by the pound. Mom picked two rows at a time. She picked on her knees when her back got tired, and not many others could do that. Picking cotton was hard on the body, but Mom said that she earned more from picking, than chopping cotton. She said, she often made $10 to $12 a day picking, but just $5 a day for chopping. This was before the 1970s. Regardless of my parents' efforts, their combined salaries didn't equal a living wage.

Despite not earning a living wage, they needed those jobs. To make ends meet, the landowner allowed them to use a small piece of land on the farm to plant and grow fruits, vegetables, and nuts. In addition, they raise chickens and pigs. The harvest produced an abundance of food, which they shared with family members, friends, the landowner, and others.

As late as the early 1970s, Black school-aged children from impoverished families were expected to follow in their parents' footsteps. Many of these students worked in the fields, or other parts of the cotton industry from April through November every year. But Mom and Dad kept us in school for the entire school year, September through May. Mom said, "Education is the key to a better life." Many years later, I learned that this was their form of activism. They knew that education was key to ending a life of poverty and servitude. In doing this, they risked the wrath of the landowner.

When I was fourteen, the landowner fired my father. It was one or two weeks before the Christmas Holiday. Just like that, we were homeless. My siblings and I had grown up on that farm, and in that old house. That's how it was, Dad was no longer needed. He said that the landowner said to him, "I am planning for retirement, and I don't need two tractor drivers. I sold my other property, and that driver will move into this house. You have to be gone by New Year's Day."

Tractor drivers didn't usually look for work in the winter, because there was no work for them to do. It wouldn't be easy for Dad to find a new job. Complicating his search, the Christmas Holiday Season.

Mom said to Dad, "Ask him to give you more time to find a place to go.

Dad responded later, that the landowner told him, "I don't care where you go, but you best be gone by the first of the month."

Mom shared our unfortunate situation with her family, and glory be to God, a family member gave Dad a lead on a job and a recommendation. Dad got the new job, which included a bigger house for his family, and homelessness averted. But that year, there was no money for Christmas gifts. Mom said, "We had to be grateful for what we had received." For Christmas, we had good food, each other, and some great memories. The following are two of my favorite memories.

One year, Mom bought Jack a fancy red fire engine. She

was so proud of that purchase. She said, "The fire engine cost $12, I put it on layaway, and finished paying for it just in time for Christmas. White families bought this kind of toy for their kids." It was pretty. But, six months later, her favorite child, Jack, decided to destroy it in a fit of pretend rage. He used rocks, dirt, his foot, anything he could find to wreck it. When he finished, the red fire engine, looked like an elephant stepped on it. When Mom saw it, she cried. Jack lied and said, "Dakota did it." Jack was covered in dirt, so she knew he had lied. She got a thin green switch and wore Jack's butt out.

He screamed so loud that a neighbor, an old man, living across the bayou, ran to our house to see what was going on. The old man, begged Mom to stop whipping Jack, but she ignored him. Continued with her madness, and Jack continued waling and trying to escape. The old man pleaded some more to Mom, to let Jack go. But she wouldn't. Finally, the old man left shaking his head saying, "That boy didn't do nothing to deserve all that." Mom continued to warm up Jack's backside with that thin switch. I wanted to laugh at Jack, but Mom was so mad, I was scared, and thought she might change her mind and whip me too.

Another fun Christmas memory was when Mom bought a tall, White, walking doll for the baby of the family. She said, "It was expensive, and I wanted to get something special for baby Glenda." Mom was again very proud of herself for being able to buy something that she said, "White families bought for their children." She said, "I put it on layaway as soon as I saw it."

We helped Glenda unwrap it. The doll was taller than her,

and it looked like a five-year-old White child. We read the instructions on how to make it walk. Jack raised one arm of the doll, and it began to walk. It moved like a robot. It had no flexibility in its legs. It walked towards Glenda with one arm raised. All of a sudden, Glenda's facial muscles tightened, her nose wrinkled up, and she let out an earsplitting scream. Then, she ran and hid behind Mom. The giant marching monster walked right past her into the wall. It stood there, legs still moving as it would eventually walk through that wall. Glenda was not impressed. She was wailing as Mom watched speechless. My siblings and I were laughing so hard, we hadn't noticed how bewildered Mom looked.

Poor Mom, once again, her good intention to do something special for her children had gone awry. Tears were in Mom's eyes. She looked so sad, her jowls sagged. It looked as if the skin would drop off her beautiful face. Glenda didn't like her special gift. Actually, she was afraid of the big, White, walking doll. She never got comfortable with it, and didn't play with it. The older children roughhoused with the doll, and before long, the giant magic walking doll had disappeared. These tales of Christmas past are fun childhood memories my siblings and I happily share about, and with each other.

Chapter 8

The Devil We Didn't Know

With my $1 allowance in hand, I skipped to the drugstore to buy a new book and a soft- serve ice cream cone. A friend told me that the drugstore sold better books and ice cream than the grocery store. I stepped inside, everyone turned and stared at me. Their eyes piercing, like X-ray vision, burned holes in my soul. Fear gripped me. *What did I do?* My feet couldn't move, It felt like a bucket of cement had been poured on them. The owner hurried from behind the counter, her eyes a blaze and never leaving mind, she stopped, and leaned forward inches from my face. *How did she do that? She must be a witch, and she rode an invisible broom. I've never seen an old lady move that fast.*

She asked in a mean voice, "What do you want?"

"I want to buy a book and a soft-serve ice cream," I said in my weakest childlike voice. I was trembling. The smell of onions on her breath made me nauseated. She looked at the books in the nearby bookcase, randomly chose one with a cute baby deer on the cover, and handed it to me. "I don't want that one," I said.

She glared at me and snatched the $1 bill from my hand. Ouch! I winced and snatched my hand back. She had scratched me, but didn't pause to notice. She rushed back behind the counter as quickly as she had approached me. I was frozen in place, and wondered why my friends hadn't told me that the drugstore owner was mean. They acted as if it was okay for Black people to shop there. I planned to tell them to never send anyone else to this place, because Black folks weren't welcome there.

It was a Saturday afternoon, and the drugstore was packed with White teenagers and young adults enjoying the comfort of an air conditioner, their friends, beverages, and food. They were obviously children of privilege, the sons and daughters of bankers, landowners, lawyers, doctors, and other business elites. The patrons who had been watching the show abandoned me, and left me to my fate. Their eyes and minds returned to what they were doing before my naivety had disturbed them. The hum of the air conditioner reminded me that my chill was not caused by fear alone, but also by the cold air coming from the air conditioner. My summer dress offered no protection from the blizzard coming from that big machine in the window.

The mean old lady returned with a small cone of soft-serve ice cream and my change. Holding the book up, again, I said in a soft voice, "I don't want this book." The mean old woman put one hand on her hip, and with the other, she pointed to the door. I was happy to leave but disappointed with the purchases, and upset at how the old woman had treated me. I hurried off to find Mom.

Seeing Mom, I said, "The old lady in the drugstore was mean to me, and look what she did." I showed Mom the scratch on my hand. She looked at it, poured water over my hand, and wrapped it with a handkerchief from her purse.

"You'll be okay, but stay out of the drugstore. That old women, and her brother are not nice people. She could cause us a lot of trouble," Mom said.

"Okay, Mommy."

That was a teachable moment, and an important lesson well learned—don't ever spend money in a place where you are not welcome, or treated with kindness and respect. That's my mantra for life.

The Ku Klux Klan (KKK) was very visible and busy during the Civil Rights Movement. Their reputation was built on extreme violence. Just the mention of the KKK, caused fear and many sleepless nights for people of color. The devil we didn't know hid behind robes and hoods and burned down homes, businesses, and churches. They killed children of color and instilled fear in others. The KKK operated anonymously, and had the freedom to enforce illegal Jim Crow laws in the Deep South. Despite all those roadblocks and evil acts of violence, the Movement kept on moving.

Aunt Cora, my father's youngest sister, told me when she was about ninety that she wanted to clarify a story that had been erroneously attributed to my father. She said, "My son Hank had an interracial relationship with the landowner's daughter, and he got the girl pregnant. The White girl was about fourteen at the time. Black and White relationships were illegal in the

State of Mississippi. The KKK showed up one night and parked with their headlights directed at the house. The man who did the talking must have been the leader. He said, 'Cora, you come on out here now. I want to talk to you.' I took my time getting to the porch because I was scared. But I wondered how he knew that I was the head of the house, and that there was no husband in there. We had to be careful around White folks, because you never knew who's under those sheets, hoods, or capes. The lights blinded me, I saw only shadows of about ten men, all covered up, standing by their vehicles.

The leader said, 'You know why we're here. Send that boy out here.'

I said, 'Please sir, don't hurt us. He ain't here. He left earlier today, and said he wasn't coming back.'

The man was quite, and that made me nervous. I stood there like a stone too afraid to move a muscle. After a few tense minutes, the leader broke the silence, and said, 'He better not come back here, because if he does, it's going to be bad for all of you.'

I said, 'Yes sir, thank you sir. He won't be coming back here.'

We didn't sleep at all that night. We were too afraid that they would come back and burn the house down. I knew that we had gotten off light for what Hank and that girl had done. The Lord blessed us from evil that night. But I had to pray for forgiveness, because I had to lie to the KKK to save my son. Hank was inside hiding way back under the bed. Thank God they didn't decide to come into the house that night. We couldn't have stopped them, and it would have been real bad for all of us. Only the Lord knows if we would have survived.

Before dawn the next day, a family member slipped my son out of the house and took him to a neighboring town to catch a bus to California to live with my sister. Only God knows why those horrible men spared us that night. But I am forever grateful."

During this period, some of our family and friends left the Mississippi Delta to look for better housing and job opportunities, or out of fear. My uncle Jacob and his family disappeared, one night, from their home near Dawson Lake. Specifically, during the time of the Civil Rights Movement, Blacks disappeared on their own accord, and didn't tell other family members for fear that their plans might be leaked. Mom was scared because it was also common for evil to be at play when Blacks abruptly disappeared. Rose and I were scared, because his daughters were our playmates.

Rumor had it that Uncle Jacob had been seen by a town official at a voter registering site. Mom didn't know if that was true, but she said, "Something must have happened for them to up and leave that way."

After what seemed to be a long time, Mom told us, "Finally, I got a letter from Jacob and his wife today. They're in Missouri and doing well. Thank the Lord."

We never saw them again. Hate is an awful spirit that kills, destroys families, and steals dreams. People are not born with the spirit of hate. It's a learned behavior. To this day, I don't understand why people teach hate. Despite how my parents were treated, they never taught us to hate anyone.

Chapter 9

They Chose Salvation

It was the summer of 1968, I was thirteen and Rose was sixteen. Mom informed us, "It's time for you two to get to know the Lord. Revival begins Friday night at the little church on the Landrum farm."

The landowner donated an old house to the Black people who lived on his farm. They made modifications to make it look like a church. It sat off a dirt road surrounded by a cotton field. They found a preacher, and hosted services one Sunday a month. For revival, the preacher would be there three consecutive Fridays, and a Sunday.

There were three candidates seeking salvation—Rose, me, and a teenage boy from a nearby farm. We sat on what was called the mourners' bench, which was placed in a prominent spot in the church so everyone could see us. The preaching and praying were for us. After each sermon, the preacher extended his hand and asked, "Are you ready to receive Jesus Christ as your Lord and Savior?" When he had finished his second Friday night of preaching, praising, and praying, the teenage boy and Rose stood and took the preacher's hand, acknowledging that they were ready to accept Jesus Christ as their Lord and Savior. The preacher preached harder and louder, but I wouldn't take his hand. After he closed the service that night, he said to me, "You need to pray more in the coming week, and tell your parents they need to come to church next Friday night to give you some support."

During the week, I prayed, and asked the Lord to give me a sign when it was my time to receive Him as my Lord and Savior. Friday night, the last night of revival, Dad attended church with us. Everyone was happy to see him. They gave him a seat facing me. The service started, and a deacon asked Dad, "Would you like to pray for your daughter?" Dad could be very shy, and that was one of those times. He crossed his legs and folded his arms a few times, and said, "Naw. Y'all go ahead. Maybe next time." I felt so sorry for him. I couldn't believe they had shamed him. He wasn't a churchgoing man, I was surprised when he decided to come with us, instead of Mom. Dad should have been on that mourner's bench with me. I bet Satan was jumping up and down, because he knew it would be a long time before my father entered a church again. I wished that I had faked it, and gotten up the week before. If I had, this wouldn't have happened to him.

The deacons prayed, and everyone sang the worship hymns "Amazing Grace" and "Precious Lord." The service was electric. The preacher put on a show, he preached louder than I'd ever heard before. He shouted, jumped, stomped his feet, and leaned forward and backward while praising the Lord. He was wet with sweat. The small congregation enjoyed his performance. They were on their feet trying to fan him, and encourage him on. All the activity distracted me. *Does it take all this to get me to salvation?* He scared me when he stomped his feet, and raised his voice, I winced. When he approached me, I winced again. He put his hand on my head, and began to pray. That made me uncomfortable. I looked at Dad for comfort, but he wouldn't make eye contact with me. I didn't like anyone touching my head, but there he was doing that. *I prayed, Lord, please forgive me for I have sinned because I want to punch the preacher for violating my personal space. Oh, my goodness, I felt something. I think, that's it. The Holy Spirit stirred in my soul.*

When the preacher concluded his sermon, wiped his face with his handkerchief, and approached me with his outstretched hand, I stood and took it. The little church erupted in applause, hallelujahs, and praises to the Lord. They sang and thanked the Lord. A woman behind me whispered to another woman, "I thought she'd be back here next year." I smiled, because that had been a distinct possibility.

The preacher announced the location of the baptism—Dawson Lake the coming Sunday at 10:00 a.m. I couldn't believe they had chosen that location. They must not know how bad the snakes were in that lake. Mom loved to fish in Dawson Lake, and I witnessed the snakes chase her away from her favorite fishing spots.

I said, "Mom the baptism is going to be in Dawson Lake. You know how bad the snakes are there?"

Dad responded, "They know how to find a spot that will be free of snakes and safe for y'all."

Mom asked me, "Did you get religion tonight?"

"Yes," I said.

"Then you don't have anything to worry about."

Parents say the most interesting things. When they don't want to validate your concerns. I witnessed the aggressiveness of the snakes in Dawson Lake, and now they wanted us to get in that water. Much doubt and confusion swirled around in my head. We are going to need a miracle on Sunday morning.

At about 10:00 Sunday morning, the three candidates for baptism arrived at the lake wearing long white cotton gowns. Rose and I wore pants underneath our gowns to avoid showing too much, if our legs went up, when they dipped us in the water. The preacher and the deacons were already in the water singing and praying. I hoped that they had prayed away all those snakes. There were other church members in the water, they formed a line that led to the preacher and the deacons. They assisted the candidates in and out of the water. They were wearing white robes too. Seeing all of those peoples in the water made me feel a little better, but still not totally convinced that this was a safe plan. Since nothing happened to them, maybe we would be okay.

As it turned out, the Lord made a path for us, and blocked satan from crossing it. We were born again that day. We left our old, sinful spirits in Dawson Lake, and walked out of the water born again in Christ Jesus.

Soon after, local churches stopped performing baptisms in the lake. Church leaders, figured out how to conduct water baptism indoors.

Chapter 10

Finding Courage

The traumatic events and exposure to extreme violence during my childhood caused fear and self-doubt. Getting connected in a local church helped me overcome many of the problems that took hold in my youth. Learning to forgive was an essential part of my early religious training. Through forgiveness, I found courage and confidence. With courage, my future looked attainable.

My seventeenth birthday ushered in my senior year of high school. My visions of bigger and better things for the future were near. Mom said, "Prepare properly and success will come if you don't give up." But before I realized it, an old friend reappeared—fear. That made me nervous and caused stress, because at that point, I hadn't yet developed an escape plan for myself. Doubt crept into my mind about whether a high school diploma would be enough to allow me to avoid institutional racism and poverty. College was not an option for me. Because, attending college, at that time, would have been an added burden on my parents. My goal was to help them, and my future didn't include working in the hot cotton fields, or as a domestic.

As I daydreamed in class one day, the answer came to me—I can enlist in the military. I was so excited that I made an awkward move, and my pencil rolled off my desk. I leaned over to pick it up, and the teacher asked, "Dakota, do you have something to add?" (The class erupted in laughter.) With knots in my throat, I said, No," and then hid behind the student sitting in front of me. I thought of all the benefits of enlisting—immediate independence, a living wage, travel, learn a skill, and save money for college. Enlisting would allow me to do good for myself, my family, and my country. I would be a superhero of sorts slaying one dragon at a time.

Knowing nothing about women in the military, I had to research the matter before I shared the plan with my parents. Later that week, I dropped in to see the school guidance counselor, and saw a pamphlet with a woman smartly dressed in a military uniform on the cover. It was a recruitment pamphlet for the US Army, Women's Army Corps. The counselor saw me looking at the pamphlet and asked, "Are you interested?"

"Yes, I think so," I said.

"We haven't had any women from this high school join the military," he said.

He contacted a recruiter to determine my qualifications. After I completed the entrance and physical examinations, I had to graduate high school, and be at least seventeen with a parent's signature, or have turned eighteen before the official date of enlistment.

A week passed, as I struggled with how to tell my parents. They need to hear it from me, before someone else told them. News like this, traveled fast in our small community. My parents had reconciled, after being separated for more than six months, and I wanted to present this news in a way that wouldn't create a problem for them. I decided to tell them on a Thursday night, and then, tell my friends on Friday.

While I was doing the dishes, my hands were shaking, and a dish slipped out of my hand and broke into pieces. All eyes were on me. After composing myself, I blurted out, "Mom and Dad, I'm going into the Army." Mom lowered her eyes and began squeezing her hands. She didn't speak. Dad's jaw tightened, he scratched his face, crossed his legs, and looked at me. "Where did you get that idea?" he asked.

"I read about it in a book."

After a deep sigh, he said, "When I was in service, I didn't have any contact with military women. Let's have a conversation with your godfather to get his opinion on the matter."

My godfather had served in the US Navy during World War II, and I hoped he would be able to answer questions that my parents had about women in the military, and maybe tell me more about it too.

A few days later, we stopped by his house. As Dad was explaining the reason for our visit, I saw the muscles in my godfather's right hand, right arm and his jaw tightened up. He cleared his throat and spit. He turned around and his eyes were glowing. He said in a voice that I didn't recognize, "Women don't belong in the military. The men don't respect women in the military. It's too dangerous and unsafe especially for a young girl like her." My godfather was about eighty, at that time. I had never seen him so upset. Mom and Dad appeared to be in a state of shock.

I calmly said, "I know how to take care of myself. This won't change me. I'll be the same person I am now."

His voice grew angrier and louder. "You're too young and naive to know better or understand the magnitude of this decision. I don't agree, and I don't support it."

His unexpected reaction caught me, and my parents off guard. Dad thanked him for his time, and we began the drive home. My father's jaw was tense, and it sounded like he was grinding his teeth. Mom was quiet. The silence was awful between us. The noise from the gravel tapping the undersides of the car, almost made the ride home palpable. In the background, a song that I recognized began to play on the car radio, and it became an even better alternative for the silence.

I thought that my godfather would have been on my side, but I was wrong. My spirit had never been so blue. I wondered what my parents would say. They respected my godfather, and they are probably going to side with him. I folded my arms across my chest and breathe a long sigh of despair.

This time the ride home appeared to take longer, and I was miserable, in the backseat all alone, waiting for my parents to speak. We had to cross the old Dawson Lake Bridge to get home. I hated that bridge, and became overwhelmed with fear, whenever I had to cross it. From the backseat, I willed Dad to increase his speed, so we could get off the bridge faster, but he continued to drive like a snail. That day, the noise from the old bridge appeared to be extra loud, and creepier than before. To endure this, it was a punishment all by itself. One day, the old bridge would collapse, and I hoped that we wouldn't be on it when it happened.

The bridge appeared to have been built more than a hundred years earlier. It had one lane, and traffic flowed either north or south. The first vehicle on the bridge had the right of way. Every type of machinery—big combines, tractors, road graders, school buses, tractors pulling trailers packed with cotton, and tractor trailers loaded with cows, used the old bridge.

Because the bridge crossing was taking such a long time, my mind wondered off to the lone, weatherworn, and abandoned grave marker that overlooked Dawson Lake. The marker was enclosed by a delicate wire fence, with the date of 1857 still visible, and located near the south entrance to bridge. The site was not a Native American burial. The county was formed in 1844. Based on the size of the headstone, it must have been the grave of a wealthy early settler to the area, or maybe Dawson himself. As a young child, my friends and I played near the site. It spooked us, but that didn't stop our curiosity.

That old headstone raised a lot of questions—*Why would someone choose that location to bury a person? Who was buried there? Did the person buried there haunt drivers crossing the bridge?* As I thought about that last question, a memory came to mind about a paranormal experience that cousin Roberta reported. One

Saturday evening before dark, Roberta returned to our house driving at a high rate of speed. We could hear the sound of gravel hitting the undercarriage of the car, as a thick cloud of dust followed behind. She slammed on the brakes, the car fished tailed before it stopped in front of our house. The cloud of dust that followed her car, engulfed it. We coughed, and used our hands to fan away the dust. When Roberta stepped out of the car, she was in a complete state of panic - eyes wide; breathing labored; body trembled, and her mouth quivered, as she kept mumbling, "I saw granddaddy."

We were concerned about Roberta's behavior. Mom asked her, "What happened after you left here a short time ago?" Roberta said, "As I approached the bridge, I looked in the rearview mirror, and saw granddaddy sitting in the middle of the back seat." Mom assured her that grandfather loved her, and that he wouldn't do anything to harm her, or cause her to harm herself. After about thirty minutes, she had calmed enough to drive, because she didn't like driving after dark.

Dad cleared his throat, and that interrupted my thoughts about ghosts and such. We crossed the bridge, and our house was now visible in the distance. Dad said, "We respect your godfather's opinion. If you're determined to enlist, you'll have to wait until you turn eighteen. Then you can make your own decision."

Overwhelmed with joy, I couldn't utter a word. My spirit took wings, left the car, and flew ahead of them singing and dancing like a hummingbird all the way home.

Chapter 11

I Have Decided

My great escape to a lifetime of grand adventures was near. When some of my friends learned about my big plans, they were interested too. They shared the news with their friends, who spread the news further. That resulted in about twenty-five women from my high school class volunteering to enlist in the US Army, Women's Army Corps. To my surprise, most of these women enlisted in a program called the Buddy Plan. This program allowed new recruits to enlist with friends, and train together. When we graduated in mid-May of that year, they departed for basic training, leaving me behind, because I was not yet eighteen.

Disappointed that they wouldn't delay their departure to allow me to travel and train with them, I threw myself a pity party. But then I realized that we had different goals, and therefore, our paths would not be the same. I began this journey alone, and I may have to finish it alone. Despite the fact that

I had never been more than a hundred miles from home, the real world beckoned. I learned about the world beyond my home state by reading books, and I loved imaginary adventures. But this journey would be real-life, and I must get prepared mentally and physically. There were still many questions that I needed to find answers to, before I embarked on the journey that would change my life.

I worried about not liking the food that would be cooked by other people. I grew up on a farm, but my palate was very selective. Mom knew what I liked, and didn't like. She made sure that there was something good for me to eat all the time. Everyone loved her cooking and especially her flakey biscuits, blackberry and peach cobblers. She made the moistest cakes and the juiciest chicken. The butterflies in my stomach were telling me that the food served in the US Army wouldn't be like Mom's.

The thought of flying for the first time worried me a little, because Mom raised concerns and fears when I expressed interest in becoming a stewardess. Worrying was not going to help me, it would only hurt. Life had prepared me for the good times and the not so good. When the time comes for me to depart, I would be ready to do what was uncomfortable.

Two months after my eighteenth birthday, my orders and an airplane ticket arrived with instructions to report to my first military assignment, basic training in Alabama.

Chapter 12

It's Time to Go

Mom and several of my siblings accompanied me to the airport. It was raining, and I hoped that the flight would be canceled. But then, someone announced the arrival of the aircraft. We went to the large windows to watch it land. When it first appeared below the clouds, it looked very small, but as it got closer and closer, it got bigger and bigger. We watched in amazement until it landed and made its way to the boarding area.

It was time for me to board the aircraft. My family was generous with hugs and kisses. My father was absent. Work took priority, despite the rain. I thought that he would be there, since I was doing something no other woman in our family had done before. I felt overwhelmed, my stomach knotted up, and my palms were sweaty. As I walked to the airplane, all eyes were on me. The weight of my decision made my whole body feel heavy. I had to mentally demand my feet to keep moving me forward. I refused to look back. I had to prove to myself, and to my family that there wasn't anything to worry about.

I boarded the airplane, found my seat in the no-smoking section, and fastened my seat belt. I looked out the window, waved and blew kisses to my family. They waved back. Mom took a handkerchief from her purse to wipe her tears. My tears began to flow freely. I didn't want to leave my family. But I had too, because the life that I wanted for myself, wasn't available in my home state. Plus, Mom and Dad had separated again, and it looked like they would divorce. She would need my help more than ever now, because she was expecting a baby. Despite the reconciliation and the pregnancy, the domestic violence had continued.

One of the worst incidents of domestic violence occurred between my parents, on a Saturday night, a few months before graduation. Mom had a date with Dad, and Rose and I, doubled dated with our boyfriends. Mom and Dad arrived home a few minutes ahead of us. We walked into the living room to find Mom laying on the floor, and I saw a demon, as black as night, with eyes of fire, and filled with rage, straddling her - with a big, long, shiny hunting knife to her throat, as he threatened to kill her. Terrified, I screamed in horror, "Get off her. Get off her. I hate you. I hate you." This was the last thing that I expected to see that night. Our boyfriends appeared to be in a state of shock. They looked like flag poles, because they were standing so straight. Mom whispered, "Go get the police." Rose's boyfriend said, "Mr. Land, please don't hurt her." The demon was disguised as my father. He ignored our pleas, and remained in his saddle, like she was a horse, as he brandished that big shiny blade readying it to take the life of a helpless woman in front of her children.

My boyfriend, grabbed my hand and pulled me towards the front door, and said, "Let's go get the police." "No, I don't want to go. Why don't you do something to help her? Mom could be dead by the time we returned," I said. The twenty-mile drive back to town felt like a hundred. I hid my face in my hands as I cried in anguish. No one talked. The only noise that I heard, was the sound of the car's engine and myself wailing.

The town's first Black policeman was our cousin on Mom's side of the family. He wasn't hard to find that night. He was parked under a street light, on the corner facing main street, near the Black owned jukes, gambling establishments, and cafes. Rose and her boyfriend told him what we had witnessed back at our house. With sirens blaring and lights flashing, he led the way, as we followed close behind. The trip back, took a lot less time than it did going into town.

The policeman entered the house first. Mom was sitting on the coach, she had visible red marks around her neck where the knife had been. She was not dead, but her skin was as white as a sheet. She must have seen Jesus when the demon had his knife to her throat. *What made him do that? Satan had nothing on my father.*

The policeman asked, "Where is he?"

"He ran out of here into one of those cotton fields," Mom replied.

"I'll go look for him," he responded.

The policeman drove a short distance down the dirt road,

disappearing into the darkness of the night, and shined his search light from his vehicle, into the field on both sides of the road. The cotton was about four feet high with thick, and green foliage. The policeman had no chance of spotting Dad under those conditions, unless he stood upright. *"Why didn't he get out of the car, and try looking for him on foot?"* A short time later, the policeman returned, and said to Mom, "Don't worry, he probably won't be back tonight."

I said, "Probably? What are we supposed to do if he does?"

He responded, "He will have cooled off by then. But now, there is nothing more I can do here tonight."

I was at a loss for words. Dad had never been arrested for any of the bad things that he had done to Mom. That night was no exception.

The policeman, and our boyfriends left us alone to fend for ourselves against the grey eyed monster. I slept in my street clothes for weeks after that night, fearing that in the wee hours of the morning, Dad would act on his threat to kill Mom, and I would have to run to a neighbor's house to get help.

Monday was a school day, and it came too soon. I dreaded having to go back, because I feared that everyone on campus would know the deep dark family secret that had been hidden from public eye, until now. I was embarrassed, ashamed and spiritually broken, because someone, outside of our household, had witnessed the horror that I had lived with all of my life. I was traumatized, and had no desire to communicate with my boyfriend, or anyone else. I withdrew like a turtle, and kept to myself, for fear of having to speak about that awful night.

A year earlier, Rose had move out, but had come home that weekend for a visit. She went back to her new life, and we are yet to speak of the horrors of that Saturday night.

Dad returned home the next day. Things were very different between my parents. They slept in separate rooms, and Dad stopped eating Mom's cooking. He claimed, Mom was trying to poison him. Every meal that she prepared for him, he tossed to the dogs. The dogs got fat, and Dad got skinny. I became jealous of the dogs. They ate better than us children. Mom put the best part of the meat on Dad's plate. She gave us the less favorable cuts, with lots of vegetable, potatoes and gravy.

About two months after the policeman's visit to our house, I came home from school to find Mom had packed up the whole house. She announced to us kids, "We are moving, and your father is not coming with us." I was beyond happy. I didn't ask where we were going, because I didn't care. I just didn't want to live with my father.

I loved my parents, but I didn't like them as a couple. Mom was visibly sadden over the break up, but I prayed they would learn that they were better apart, than they had ever been together.

Under the circumstances, the timing of my departure for basic military training didn't feel right. But, I didn't know enough about the military to try and change my orders. Plus, I needed to make some real money.

The stewardess, speaking over the airplane's intercom, brought me back to reality. The aircraft started to move and picked up speed. We lifted off and were soon in the clouds.

Exhaling deeply, I prayed, *Heavenly Father, please calm my mom's thoughts and fears. Hold her in your loving arms until I can hug her again. Most of all, please, heavenly Father, put a cover of protection around this aircraft and lend us your mightiest Angel to guide us safely to our destination. In the mighty name of Jesus, I pray, amen.*

After the prayer, I began to relax. I was doing very well, and I hadn't reached for the barf bag. I mentally applauded myself—Look at me!

The military had not been my first choice for a career. I wanted to be a flight attendant—a stewardess, as the position was called in the early 1970s. Mom had disapproved of the idea. She said, "Every time an airplane went down, I'd think it was yours." I had respected her decision, and looked for something else to do with my life. Little did we know, at the time, that the major mode of transportation for military personnel would be air travel, and with that, the risk could be higher.

We landed at Atlanta's international airport. I was startled by the size of the facility. It looked like a small city—so many airplanes of all sizes and thousands of people, more than I had ever seen before in one place. People were boarding and getting off airplanes, eating in restaurants, and standing around chatting. It was noisy. All of those commingled conversations were interesting to hear.

The smell of food reminded me that I hadn't eaten since breakfast, but I didn't dare stop for food for fear of missing my second flight. I ignored my stomach's growling. But coming in my direction were a large number stewardesses, this caught my eye. Mesmerized by their beauty and sophistication, they looked like fashion models on a runway. They walked in groups of two or more, each group were more elegantly dressed than the others. The moment took me back to when I aspired to become a stewardess. Several of them acknowledged my inquiring eyes, and smiled warmly at me. *Did they know they were living my dream? Where in the world are they going?*

Impressed by this encounter, I hadn't remember anything special about the single stewardess who worked my first flight, and that made me sad. It also brought me back to reality.

I had lost track of time, and I didn't know if I was heading in the right direction. My stress level rose. Then I remembered Mom's instructions: "Don't be afraid to ask for help." With my ticket and handbag in hand, I looked for someone who appeared trustworthy to ask for assistance. I stopped a nice-looking man in a uniform, and he gave me directions. *Lord, let this be correct because I don't want to miss my flight.* I made it to the departure gate, confirmed the information on my ticket with the data posted at the gate, and exhaled. It had been a long walk. I was thankful that I had managed it with no problem.

To my surprise, I saw more than thirty women of different races and ethnic backgrounds waiting in the boarding area. Because of the diversity, I double checked the information on my ticket, because I didn't know if the training would be integrated. After observing them in the gate area, I concluded, these women must be going to the same military facility as me. As fate would have it, we would be together for the next eight weeks.

The second airplane arrived. It was much smaller than the first one, but there were enough seats for everyone with a few left over. This flight was shorter than the first—just forty-five minutes or less. We landed in Alabama. It was a much smaller airport, and I guessed that the town must have been small too. We got off the airplane and followed the signs to baggage claim. After claiming our luggage, we gathered near the entrance and waited for our military escort.

The escort, a young woman about five feet tall, and wearing black, shiny, tie-up loafers, a smart, crisp, lightweight skirt, and a short-sleeved jacket. She read off names from a list, and when she called out "Dakota J. Land," I responded, "Here," just as the other women had said. We were directed to a big, long bus that looked like something from World War II. It was waiting on a dark side street, engine running, the door open, and lights ablaze, it looked suspicious, a good prop for a horror movie. But in this case, the old bus was in good operating condition, and ready to transport us to the military facility, and the start of our new lives.

It had been a long and adventurous day, but it wasn't over. I was exhausted and hungry. I thought a boxed lunch and then a nap would be great about now. We boarded the bus and settled in. No snack was offered, and to my dismay, as soon as my eyes closed, the bus growled to a stop. It had taken only about ten minutes to get to the military installation.

It was about 10:00 p.m. when we were ordered off the bus. Our escort said, "You will be housed in the building with the sign Company B. Take your luggage, go inside, and select a bed." The sign portrayed an orange, sassy, and flirtatious-looking fox. *Are we going to be called the foxes?* The door was open, and the lights were on. The room was huge and lined with small unmade cots, with linen stacked on top, and a foot locker at the foot of each. The escort informed us that lights would be out in about an hour, and that the wake-up call would be at 5:00 a.m.

As one of the first recruits to exit the bus, my instincts led me to a cot in the back of the enormous room. Many other recruits appeared to know each other and were looking for cots closer together. There were four other Black women, and they appeared to look for cots near each other too. As luck would have it, they selected cots near me. Some of them may have enlisted on the Buddy Plan, but at that hour, my senses had slowed way down, and thinking about the sleeping arrangements of the other recruits was too difficult. I covered my mattress, and crawled between the sheets. Some made their beds, but most didn't, they acted like it was a slumber party, and they laid on top of their mattresses. Sleep came quickly.

Chapter 13

A New Beginning—
In the Army Now

Clang. Clang. Clang. Clang. Clang! I rolled off my bed onto the floor, and peeked from underneath it, towards the sound of the noise, hoping to see what was happening. Some of the women sat up in their beds, and looked confused, others stood near their beds, and looked bewildered, and some were staggering around, asking, "What's going on?"

Two women in uniform were walking in the big, open space, clanging what looked like the lids of thirty-gallon garbage cans. *What are they doing? Why are they doing this? They know we didn't get to bed until late last night.* My heart was racing, and I was breathing hard. I was scared. The surprise wakeup call, threw me right back into the chaos of my father's house.

I recognized one of the uniformed women, but not the other, who yelled, "Wake up. Get up. Recruits, you have forty minutes to make your beds, shower, dress, and get outside, and line up facing the building."

Some recruits were still asking, "What's going on?" Those who thought they understood the instructions tried to explain it to them. It was chaos. My ears were ringing, and my heart was racing. I stood, and watched about twenty women rush to get in line for the shower room. Looking at the time, I realized that a shower was not in the cards for me that morning. With the time remaining, I decided to get dressed, make my bed, and tidy up my area.

The women who had slept near me appeared to make the same decision. We were the first ones outside in line. Most of the women made it outside on time, but others were still stumbling outside at 5:40 a.m. It was a sight to behold—the late arrivals were moving as if they were drunk. Most of the recruits were in the same clothes they had worn the day before, which was my case too. Some recruits' hair were still wet or uncombed. My hair needed to be picked and patted, but that would have taken too much time. One recruit's hair looked combed and neatly styled. But she smartly donned a wig.

The beds were haphazardly made, and clothes not worn were left untidily on beds, and the floor. We didn't have time to do anytime correctly. I thought about the last forty minutes, and concluded that this was a joke, and that at any minute, someone would appear and scream, "Surprise." We would laugh about it, go back inside, and return to bed.

The two uniformed women were standing on the porch of the building looking down at us. They introduced themselves as Drill Sergeant White and Drill Sergeant Mitchell. The senior of the two was Drill Sergeant White, and she said, "Welcome to the United States Army, Women Army Corps, Company B, 1st Platoon, 2nd Battalion. Starting today, you will be called privates. You will call us drill sergeants. For the next eight weeks, we will be your sister, brother, best friend, husband, mommy, and daddy. We'll teach you everything you need to know about the Corps, and the United States Army.

During the next few days, you'll be issued military clothing for every aspect of your new life. We will instruct you on how to dress, when to eat, when to sleep, how to make your bed, and when to wake up. We will teach you how to march and how to sing. Failure to obey or follow orders may result in disciplinary actions. At the end of eight weeks, you will be able to jump higher, walk and run faster, sing louder, stand and march longer, perform self-defense and lifesaving skills, and be basic combat ready. Also, you will be the best, the smartest, and the most physically fit platoon come graduation. However, at the moment, we don't see any superheroes or anyone in this group who will make it past week three."

After hearing that last sentence, a big lump formed in my throat. My thoughts raced. *Why would she say such a thing? Why would they inject failure on day one? Failure, not an option for me. I'll have to work extra hard to prove myself. My future begins here. No going back.*

I didn't realize that my thoughts had caused my body to do something weird, and had gotten Drill Sergeant White's attention. Before I knew it, she was standing in front of me looking up into my face. "Well look-a-there," she said. "You want your mommy or daddy?" she asked me sarcastically. "Let me guess. You're thinking, you've already earned your cape, and you can just fly right on out of here, right?"

The verbal thrashing continued. Thank goodness no one laughed. I was embarrassed beyond measure. My eyes filled with tears. "Oh, we have a baby in the group. No, we have a crybaby," Drill Sergeant White said. She walked away, shaking her head. My father had warned me, "Keep your mouth shut and you'll stay out of trouble," but he hadn't said anything about my thoughts getting me into trouble. From that day forward, I realized that body language mattered too. (The crybaby tag stuck, and I would carry it throughout the eight weeks of training.)

Drill Sergeant White informed us that we were going to march to the mess hall for breakfast. Both drill sergeants moved to the left of the platoon, and Drill Sergeant Mitchell said in a loud voice, "Attention," and in the next breath, she said, "Column left." We didn't know what that meant, some of us turned left, and others right, and some didn't move at all. The drill sergeants looked surprised at our awkward responses. Then they demonstrated the commands, and on the command, forward march, we began walking forward, but not as a unit. We skipped, tripped, and stepped on the heels of others. Drill Sergeant Mitchell began calling a cadence: "Left, left, your left, right left. Your left, your left, your left right left." By the time we arrived at the mess hall—also referred to as the dining facility, dining room, or chow hall, the platoon was, somewhat, in step with the drill sergeants.

The aroma of the food met us a few blocks away from the mess hall. The butterflies woke up in my stomach, and reminded me that I hadn't eaten for more than twenty-four hours. From the smell, I could clearly delineate between bacon, ham, and coffee. Breakfast was served cafeteria style, and my selections were simple—bacon, scrambled eggs, toast, milk, and orange juice. The person in front of me, a male soldier, appeared to select one of everything being served, including something he called hash. It had a thick, gray, lumpy consistency, the cook used a soup ladle to scoop the substance, and poured it all over the mound of food already on his plate. I couldn't believe my eyes. The mixture looked like the slop we fed to the pigs on the farm. The butterflies in my stomach began to flutter, and my throat tightened. Drill Sergeant White must have been watching, because right before the butterflies took flight, she appeared in front of me, with both hands on her hips. She said, "You better not do it. Go find a seat." Happy to have not embarrassed myself in front of hundreds of other soldiers. I hurried away from her, and that awful looking hash.

My stomach had to settle down before I could try to eat. After a few minutes, I took a bite of the eggs but couldn't swallow them. The eggs were thick, rubbery, and gritty—they tasted awful. Hoping that Drill Sergeant White couldn't see me, I spit the eggs into a napkin. I took a bite of toast, and a bite of bacon. The bacon was blacken and burned. It actually didn't taste like bacon either. To avoid seeing anyone eating hash, or something else equally unappealing, I focused on my plate.

A little paranoid at that point, I felt Drill Sergeant White's piercing eyes watching my every move. The last thing I wanted was for her to call me out again. I took a mental break, exhaled, and thought about home. Alabama and Mississippi were in the same time zone, so Mom would be up preparing breakfast. I wondered what she cooked—fluffy eggs, crisp bacon, and hot biscuits with butter? Did she miss me being at the table? Right then, I was missing her cooking a lot at that moment. *Lunch and dinner will have to be better than breakfast, or I just might starve.*

Back in our barracks, Drill Sergeant White addressed us. "I see some of you princesses don't like the food you're being served. You better eat it, and learn to like it, because the training will get hard, and I will not have any of you falling out, lagging, or getting sick because the food here doesn't meet your high standards."

After that warning, the drill sergeants gave us instructions on how to organize and maintain our living space, including how to make the beds. Then, they told us that an inspection would take place in two hours. I was annoyed that I couldn't get back in bed and finish sleeping. I moved like a sloth.

It was no surprise to me that no one passed the inspection. For one thing, the blankets were not tight enough for a quarter to bounce when dropped on the bed. As the drill sergeants performed that little trick, you could hear a pin drop. Because they didn't tell us about this part of the inspection. It was an impossible task. That was day one of basic training, and it was just a tease.

A few days later, we were formally fitted for our military wardrobe, tailored to fit in accordance with military regulations. We had an outfit for every occasion, including shoes and socks. To my surprise, everything fit in one duffle bag. If I had known we would be issued so many clothes, I would have left 90 percent of what I brought at home, but no one seemed to know anything about the real world of military women. My father admitted that he couldn't tell me anything about it, and the recruiter, a man, didn't tell me, or maybe he didn't know either.

After the uniforms were issued, the drill sergeants informed us about US Army Regulation hair styles. Drill Sergeant White told me, "Your afro hairstyle doesn't comply with the regulations. It's too long and too big, and you will be out of uniform, and subject to disciplinary actions unless adequate adjustments are made." The White women were advised on what was or wasn't appropriate for them too. Frustrated, after being penalized several times for being out of uniform, because of my hair, I asked a young Black woman from Chicago, if she could cut my hair in a low-profile style similar to hers. It worked. No more complaints from the drill sergeants, and my headgear fit much better too.

Chapter 14

Becoming a WAC

As a private in the United States Army, Women's Army Corps (WAC), we learned excellent time management—how to get the most out of the time we had, and to use it wisely. We learned to do what we initially thought were impossible – thirty-three women get a shower, ready the living space, and get professionally dressed all within forty minutes. The drill sergeants instructed us on how to care for our new clothes, iron, shine shoes, shine brass, prepare for inspection, clean up our personal space, and how to clean the showers and the latrine (bathroom).

We always had work to do in the barracks. We had to keep the floors, with the 1940s-era near-faded tile, spotless. We learned how to use an industrial-sized buffer to polish the floors. The buffer had a mind of its own, as it was very powerful, and it often gave the user a thorough workout. It was a raging bull. We had to sneak up on it to turn it on. Then, you had to give it just the right amount of pressure, for it to operate it smoothly. If you didn't touch it just right, it buck like a wild stallion, and would throw you off. Everyone hated it. But, when your name appeared on the duty roster for an assignment, you did it or got in trouble. There was a silver lining, once someone figured out how to calm the beast, she shared her discovery and technique with everyone else.

By week three, about half of the platoon, including myself had mastered the technique that allowed a quarter to bounce when dropped on the bed. The first day that this was demonstrated, I was a skeptic, and thought it was a trick. But, we kept at it, until we figured out how to do it. The first time my cot passed inspection, Drill Sergeant White couldn't believe it. She got on the floor and looked under my cot to see if the blanket had been altered. I mentally celebrated that victory – yes! When several of my peers passed the cot inspection, they slept on the hard floor for weeks. Because they didn't believe they could get the same results again.

We were required to get immunized. Vaccines were given for every disease imaginable. I hated the sight of needles, and I did my best to be the last person in the platoon to get immunized. Drill Sergeant White kept her eyes on me, and made it her business to embarrass me. It didn't matter where she found me in the line, she would tell me, "You better not cry." By then, the crybaby tag didn't bother me. Despite the extra attention, I was doing very well. The tears were not a sign of weakness, but of how much strength it took for me to keep my mouth shut.

A few days after a round of vaccines, I noticed a swollen,

weeping, growth about the size of a nickel, on my left arm, near the injection site of one of the vaccines. When the US Army medic saw it, he said it was a reaction to the typhoid vaccine. He mixed up a concoction and applied it to the affected area. This reminded me of the times when Mom used homeopathic medicine to help us stay healthy. He said, "This treatment will stop the growth and allow the inflamed area to heal. Don't worry. These things happened sometimes." That was not the answer that I wanted to hear, and it didn't boost my confidence, or offer encouragement to help me overcome my fear of needles.

We cleaned all the time, and this gave us the opportunity to learn about each other. Of the thirty-three women, five including me were Black, and one was of Russian descent. The platoon bonded over the fact that working together would benefit all versus each trying to make it on her own. A woman in the group who was about thirty took the younger women under her wing. She became the go-to person for questions, information, or just to talk about home.

She and a younger Black woman hailed from Chicago. Based on my observation, they were very cool. They smoked cigarettes, told adult jokes, talked about clubbing, drinking alcohol (booze), and the men they had known. I bunked near them, and never got tired of them talking, in detail, about their adventures. I had a feeling that they may have been lying about some of their exploits, but that was okay, because the stories were very entertaining.

The two other Black women were from Kansas City. They were a bit shy, but they too enjoyed the tales of the two from

Chicago. Their storytelling reminded me of my father's tall tales. No one could tell a story like him. He had a gift. You couldn't tell if he was lying or telling the truth. He could tell a lie, and make it sound as convincing as the truth. That's why I considered the women's stories just for entertainment.

The Chicagoans wanted to know why a Black girl from Mississippi had been named Dakota J. Land. I explained that Dakota came from my paternal aunt and that it paid homage to her and my Native Americans ancestors. I said that the surname Land came from my father's ancestors' enslaver.

The Chicagoans asked, "Can we call you DJ?"

"Yes," I happily replied.

Having a nickname made me feel sophisticated, and on par with the women from Chicago and Kansas City. The woman from Russia was friendly, had a great laugh, and loved Coca-Cola and black licorice, which she freely shared with the platoon. I didn't like its taste or the smell. However, an army of ants found it, invited all of their little friends to a party, and they led the drill sergeants to a footlocker stored in the basement, where a hoard of licorice was discovered. When confronted, the Russian didn't deny it. Once the ants were encouraged to move on, the drill sergeants put the footlocker filled with licorice on display for a short time, and instructed us to never bring such items into the barracks. Drill Sergeant White called the licorice, contraband, and said, it would be destroyed. The Russian had to do some extra cleaning as punishment for having the contraband. My heart broke for her, because I believed that the licorice was how she stayed connected to home. Then, I had another thought, for once, the drill sergeants had their eyes on someone else, and not me, which gave me some relief.

The other women were from all across the United States, including Puerto Rico. Only one race-related incident occurred, and it was raised by a young woman from the State of Virginia. She said that she didn't want to sleep in the same room with Black people. The incident made me feel uncomfortable, because I thought, the Black women would have to move to accommodate the woman from Virginia. Our barracks mom, the older woman from Chicago, heard about the matter, and offered to talk to the young woman about her concerns. The specifics of the discussion were not made public, but we were informed that the young woman from Virginia would be okay. I was happy to hear that the matter was resolved, but it had triggered a secret of my own.

The private from Virginia didn't want to sleep in the barracks with five Black women, because of racial prejudice. For me, it was the opposite – a big cultural difference. This was the first time that I had slept in a room, worked in concert with, or socialized with people who didn't look like me. I didn't know the military housed Blacks and Whites together. During the enlistment process, no one talked to me about integration, and I thought the military was segregated, at least when it came to housing.

In the early 1970s, Mississippi, my home state, continued to object to integration. With that mindset as my guide, plus the fact that Blacks and Whites, in my state, didn't relate to each other on a social level, my stress level was elevated. But from books, I learned that many people who lived in non-southern states actively and openly supported integration. The majority of the women in my platoon were from states considered progressive. Therefore, I chose to think positive, keep an open mind, and not allow past traumatic events, or difficult situations to overshadow this amazing opportunity.

I loved our mascot, a sassy orange fox, whose likeness had been captured on a pennant flag, and as we marched, it was raised high above the platoon—Foxy Bravo, Company B, 1st Platoon, 2nd Battalion. Always dressed in our starched, pressed, and wrinkle-free uniforms, we looked good. We sang and marched, rain or shine, to all of our assignments on the military installation. Here are two of my favorite marching songs.

1. Cadence caller: "They say in the Army the food is mighty fine. Am I right or wrong?"
    Platoon: "You're right."
    Cadence caller: "Sound off."
    Platoon: "One, two,
    Cadence caller: "Sound again."
    Platoon: "Three, four."
    Cadence caller: "Bring it on up."
    Platoon: "One, two, three, four, one, two, three, four."
2. Cadence caller: "Trainee, trainee don't feel blue, our recruiter lied to us too. Sound off."
    Platoon: "One, two, three, four; one, two, three, four…"

I loved those moments. We were soldiers in the US Army, Women's Army Corps, and I was proud of us all. The days of stepping on the heels of the person in front of you were long gone. We looked like a picture on a postcard. The platoon marched everywhere despite the heat or rain. Some women got blisters, and upset stomachs, but I did very well in the different elements. I enjoyed learning the formations and marching on the parade field, which was home to some of the meanest ants. When we stood there at attention or parade rest, we were allowed to slightly shake a leg, to hopefully encourage the ants to move on. The ant bites were the worst thing I had experienced up to that point.

Woo hoo! It was week three. No one had quit, and no one had been asked to leave. I hadn't forgotten what Drill Sergeant White said on day one, that some of us wouldn't make it to week three, or something to that affect. I wanted to yell, *Guess what, Drill Sergeant White? The entire platoon made it to week three, and we're doing great. Look at us!*

During the first few weeks, we learned mostly about the history of the WAC and the US Army, how and whom to salute, and whom not to salute, how to address an officer and a noncommissioned officer (NCO). We learned the difference between reveille and retreat, and what to do when you heard it played. We learned the history of the US Flag, and why it was honored, and we learned patriotic songs. The final weeks included physical fitness testing, field training, how to use protective equipment, and proper fit testing, CPR and first aid training, and practical skills testing, which would determine who graduated, and who would be recycled. We were ready to take on the final challenges.

My love of learning had returned, and I absorbed everything

like a sponge. After completion of the CPR and first aid exam, Drill Sergeant White announced, "The crybaby—Private Land—passed the CPR and first aid final exam. She was the only one to pass today. I expect the remainder of you to pass it tomorrow."

I hated the spotlight, and wished she hadn't made that announcement. I didn't want the other women to feel bad, or be upset with me. However, they were gracious and congratulated me, and some asked for my help, which I was happy to give them. I tutored each of them late into the evening on what I had done to pass. We used each other as practice subjects to perform chest compressions, mouth-to-mouth resuscitation, and how to administer first aid to an injured person. We had fun, and we were giggling and laughing as the learning continued past curfew. The next day, everyone else did pass. That was a great feeling.

Chapter 15

One Week to Go—Graduation

It's Saturday morning, one week before graduation, I got out of bed, tried to walk, but was unable to put weight on my left foot. I winced in pain, and hopped on one foot back to my bed. My left ankle had swollen overnight to the size of a medium orange. Private Smith, the go-to person in the platoon, saw my discomfort, and reported the problem to Drill Sergeant Mitchell. I was relieved that Drill Sergeant White had not responded. An X-ray showed that I had a mild stress fracture. The day before, I had stepped in a hole or a divot carefully hidden by the manicured grass on the parade field. At that time, I felt a deep, sharp pain near my left ankle, but it didn't last long. *No need to report it, right?*

The US Army medic wrapped my ankle in an Ace bandage, and said to elevate it with an ice pack to help reduce the swelling. He excused me from any prolonged standing, running, or walking for a few days. Technically, I had the weekend to recover. I feared that if I was slow to recover, I would be recycled.

Drill Sergeant White returned and appeared to be upset at the news. But by the time she made it to me, her mood had relaxed a bit. She asked, "Princess, are you okay? Do you have everything you need?" Her voice was sugary sweet. That time, everyone laughed, and I laughed too. It was how she said it, not totally sarcastic, not real mean—somewhere in between. Despite the medics advice, the injury wouldn't sideline me, because graduation was only a few days away, and being recycled was not in my plan.

Monday morning, I was dressed and ready to go. The swelling was down, but my ankle was still tender, and I walked with a slight limp. Drill Sergeant White said, "Private Land, return to the barracks, and Private Smith, you go with her." Smith expressed concern about this being the last week to complete some requirements before graduation. I assured her that she would be okay, and that I would help her if she needed it. Knowing that I had passed everything on the first try, I didn't have any final week requirements to complete.

Later that morning, Drill Sergeant White confirmed that we had completed all the requirements to graduate, and Private Smith would be promoted to E-2 for her leadership. I jumped off the bed, and hopped around on one foot. I laughed and cried. Drill Sergeant White looked stunned at first, then she said, "Happy to make your day, Private Land."

After receiving the graduation confirmation, my ankle felt better each day. On graduation day, I marched and celebrated with my platoon. Most important, all thirty-three women graduated. No one quit, no one got fired, or recycled. We made it to graduation together, and we accomplished every task that were presented on day one of basic training. Despite a few bumps along the way, we made it.

Immediately following the graduation ceremony, we began to depart for our next military assignments—advanced individual training at US Army facilities across the country.

My orders sent me to South Carolina. Of the thirty-three graduates, I would be traveling alone. Separation anxiety began to flood my spirit. We had been together for two months, and had bonded with each other. Now, it was time to leave, and go our separate ways. Despite the sadness, these emotions would be short lived, because I hadn't accomplished my goals.

Also, it was rumored that at the advanced individual training centers, the women had more freedom, and the classrooms, and public facilities were coed. If true, that would be quite a departure from our experience in basic training. That news excited most of the women in the platoon. But me, not so much. I needed to stay focused. Because, I had a secret that weighed heavily on my heart, and it would have to be resolved sooner, rather later.

Acknowledgments

Writing this book was a labor of love, because it brought back so many memories. A big heartfelt thank-you goes to my siblings living and deceased, for all the adventures we had growing up. I couldn't have survived without you, and you couldn't have made it without me.

Despite the difficult times we shared, we were very blessed. It was important for me to know that you was always there: Edna, Josie (deceased), Henry, Mary (deceased), Tommie (deceased), Gloria, Vicky, C.J., Christopher, and Denise. Thank you, Mom, for giving us life. You were a true Queen in this life, as you are an Angel now. To all my nieces, nephews, cousins, aunts, uncles, grandparents, and great-grandparents, you are a part of this too. Thank you for your gifts, strength, and courage.

Chloe, thank for being an amazing daughter, and for giving me the gift of becoming a grandmother. Thank you Princess Hailey and Princess Riley, for blessing me with so much love. Your curiosity and rambunctious spirit brought sunshine into my life. Benford and Jamila, thank you for being amazing parents.

A special thank-you goes out to military sisters and brother: Willie and Loretta, JR, Marquita, and Karen. You are my oldest friends, and I appreciate you for supporting me when we served in the US Army. Most of my accomplishments wouldn't have been possible without you being a part of my life.

Where would I be without friends? This thank-you goes out to E.J., Claudia, Mary, Rosie, Sharon, Paul, Edith, Marticia, and Raymond for always saying, yes, when I called. Thank you for being a best friend when I needed one.

Most of all, I thank God for grace, and a lifetime of blessings. Apologies to anyone I may have missed this time around. Be assured, you'll be acknowledged first in my next book.

Glossary

A

Army regulation: the rules and regulations by which the discipline, formations, field exercises, and movements of the army are directed and observed in one uniform system.

Attention: a military posture that involve standing upright with an assertive and correct posture, chin up, chest out, shoulders back, stomach in.

Autobiography: an account of a person's life written by that person.

B

Baptism: expresses an identification with Christ's death and resurrection—the old self was crucified with Christ through the waters of death, and now, followers of Jesus have risen with him in newness of life (Romans 6:3–11).

Barracks: a building or group of buildings where soldiers or other members of the armed forces live and work.

Bayou: a creek, secondary watercourse, or minor river that is tributary to another body of water.

Buddy Plan: a program by which friends who enlist at the same time go through basic combat training together. The program allows friends who enlist in the same job specialist to train together at Advance Individual Training as well.

Bullying: the ongoing and deliberate misuse of power in relationships through repeated verbal, physical, or social behavior that intends to cause physical, social, or psychological harm.

C

Cadence: a traditional call and response work song sung by military personnel while running or marching.

Chop cotton: to remove weeds, not the cotton, or the first hoeing that occurs after the young cotton plants become sturdy enough to withstand the process.

Civil Rights Movement: a political movement and campaign from 1954 to1968 in the United States to abolish institutional racial segregation, and disenfranchisement throughout the United States.

Corns: the thick, hardened layers of skill that develop when skin tries to protect itself against friction or pressure.

Corporal punishment: physical punishment such as spankings inflicted on a child by an adult in authority. Although it has been banned in many states, it's legal in many US states and boarding schools.

Cotton boll: the round, fluffy clumps on a cotton plant in which cotton grows on a cotton plant.

Cotton picker: a person who picks ripe cotton fiber from the plants. In modern times, a cotton picker is a machine that does the harvest faster.

COVID-19: an acute respiratory illness in humans caused by a coronavirus capable of producing severe symptoms and in some cases death especially in older people and those with underlying health conditions. It was originally identified in China in 2019 and became pandemic in 2020.

Croker Sack: a sack of a coarse material such as burlap.

D

Draft: mandatory enrollment of individuals into the armed forces.

Drill sergeant: a sergeant who trains new soldiers.

Drudgery: hard, menial, or and dull work.

E

Earsplitting: extremely loud.

H

Hoe: a long-handled gardening tool with a thin metal blade used mainly for weeding and breaking up soil.

Holy Spirit: the Spirit of God.

J

Johnson grass: a persistent perennial Mediterranean grass cultivated for hay and pasture in the US, where it also grows as a weed.

K

The Ku Klux Klan (KKK): a violent, secret fraternal society founded in 1915 in Georgia to maintain white Protestant cultural and political power.

L

Lay-by Season: describes the time of the season, and in the crop where the farmer has essentially completed all the in-row tillage and weed control. It's the farmer's last time of the season to work in the crop before the canopy closes or the crop gets too big for tractor traffic.

M

Mess hall: a room or building where groups of people, especially soldiers, eat together.

Mourners' bench: a bench or seat at the front of the church or room set apart for the mourners or penitent sinners seeking salvation.

N

NCO: a noncommissioned officer is a military officer who has not pursued a commission who has earned a position of authority by promotion through the enlisted ranks.

O

Outhouse: 1. a building separate from but located near a main building or dwelling. 2. US. a small structure used for defecating or urinating, typically having a seat with a hole over a deep pit.

P

Parade rest: a formal position assumed by a soldier in ranks in which he remains silent and motionless with the left foot twelve inches to the left of the right foot, with his weight resting equally on both feet, and with his arms clasped at his back with the palms to the rear. Rifles are held in the right hand with its butt touching the ground and muzzle inclined forward with the left hand at his back. Used as a command to assume this position.

Plow: a large farming implement with one or more blades fixed in a frame, drawn by a tractor or by animals, and used for cutting furrows in the soil and turning it over especially to prepare for the planting of seeds.

Private: the lowest rank given during basic combat training to a soldier without a four-year degree.

R

Retreat: a ceremony that shows respect to the flag and signifies the end of the duty day.

Reveille: a ceremony that shows respect to the flag; a bugle call at about sunrise signaling the first military formation of the day.

Revival: an awakening in a church or community of interest in and care for matters relating to personal religion; a service or a series of services for the purpose of effecting a religious awakening, followed by the playing of the "To the Colors."

S

Salvation: to be saved by God from the consequences of sin.

Servitude: a condition in which one lacks liberty especially to determine one's course of action or way of life.

T

Twilight: the soft glowing light from the sky when the sun is below the horizon caused by the refraction and scattering of the sun's rays from the atmosphere.

V

Voting Rights Act (1965): legislation that prohibited racial discrimination in voting.

W

Women Army Corps (WAC): the women's branch of the US Army. It was created as an auxiliary unit, the Women's Army Auxiliary Corps, in 1942, and converted to full status as the WAC in 1943. They were the first women other than nurses to serve in the army. The WAC was disestablished in 1978. After that, women in the US Army served in the same units as men though they have been allowed in or near combat situations only since 1994, when the defense secretary ordered the removal of substantial risk of capture from the list of grounds for excluding women from certain military units.

About the Author

Empowered by adversity, she persevered, and overcame huge challenges in her early life. In this book, part I of her autobiography, she shares some of the difficulties and traumatic experiences she encountered, and a few lessons learned along the way.

This book is riveting, spine-tingling, and thought-provoking. It will make you laugh and cry. Poverty, domestic violence, and racial discrimination helped in her decision making to leave her home and family, and look for better living and working conditions. She never shied away from controversy, or the chance to try something new or different.

Her spirit of adventure propelled her toward her destiny. What woman in her right mind would volunteer to join the US Army in the midst of an unpopular war? That's exactly what she did. After graduating from high school and turning eighteen, she enlisted in the Women's Army Corps of the US Army.

Her godfather didn't take that decision very well, and

she hated disappointing him, but off she went on the biggest adventure of her life. She had no idea what to expect, but she hoped it would be better than what she had left behind. She enlisted at a time when few women were in our nation's military. That was very brave of her. The military offered her the opportunity to learn skills, travel, earn a living wage, and save money for college. It was also an opportunity for her to help her family financially. *A total win for her.*

After serving six years on active duty, she decided to leave the Army life. With an honorable discharge, she headed to San Francisco, California, a place she dreamed of for most of her young life. She lived and worked in the beautiful Bay Area for more than forty years. The City by the Bay, described by many, as the most beautiful and culturally diverse place to live, and it remains her favorite place to call home. She raised a beautiful daughter, as a single mother, in a state that welcomed diversity, and encouraged and promoted risk-taking.

As a civilian, she managed projects and programs for the federal government; she worked with people of all ages, races, and social and economic backgrounds, political leaders, and other members of the public. The positions gave her the opportunity to express herself in writing and through public speaking. Most of all, her job gave her opportunities to travel, which often took her to other states, including Hawaii. Her mother enjoyed receiving phone calls from her every week from a different location across the US.

Since retiring from the federal workforce, she keeps busy volunteering at her church, retirement association, and for nonprofit organizations in the Bay Area. She loves to travel, and spends as much time as possible with her family.

She came from very humble beginnings, and overcame hardships to live life on her own terms. She looks forward to sharing more about her life experiences—the good, and the not so good—with you in future books. If you like fast-paced, real-life drama, you are going to love *Look! I Can Fly* part I of her autobiography.

CPSIA information can be obtained
at www.ICGtesting.com
Printed in the USA
LVHW100341041122
731992LV00007B/7